THE DROVER'S BOY

IRVINE HUNT is the author of seven books including the evocative *Road to Paradise* and *Norman Nicholson's Lakeland*, a prose anthology. A colourful literary life has included five years as a sub-editor for *The Daily Telegraph*, making a documentary film in Norway (after he had previously been deported), working as an English teacher in Sweden, and spending seven months walking round Spain and Portugal. He lives with his family in Cumbria.

THE DROVER'S BOY

Irvine Hunt

To the Buchanan
Family —
with Best wishes
Irvine Hunt
2010

Handstand Press

Published by Handstand Press
Eastbanks, Dent, Sedbergh Cumbria. England
LA10 5QT

First published in 2008

Cover design by Anne Weeks
Design and set by Long House Publishing Services
Printed and bound in Great Britain by CPI Antony Rowe,
Chippenham, Wilts.

ISBN-10: 0-9552009-4-6
ISBN-13: 978-0-9552009-4-6

For my wife

Acknowledgements

Many helped and gave encouragement as the tale evolved and my thanks go to Ross and Josie Baxter, Charlie Sheppard, Fiona Cox, Angela Locke, Phil and Eleanor Mason, Richard Quinlan, John Hurst, Captain C. Puxley, John and Lorna Sharp, Adrian Carroll, Donald Waugh, Stephen White, Liz Nuttall and my endearing family, Gwyn, Christian, Maisie, Kate and Kath.

CONTENTS

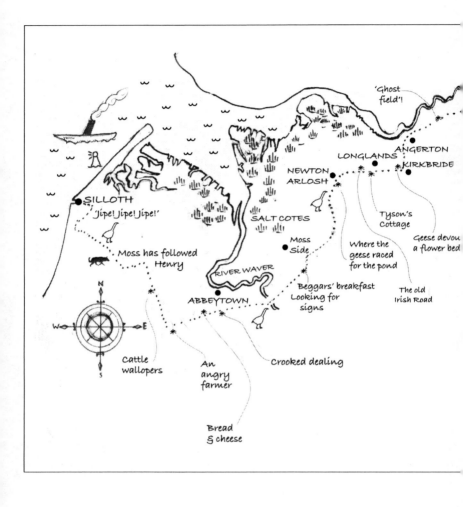

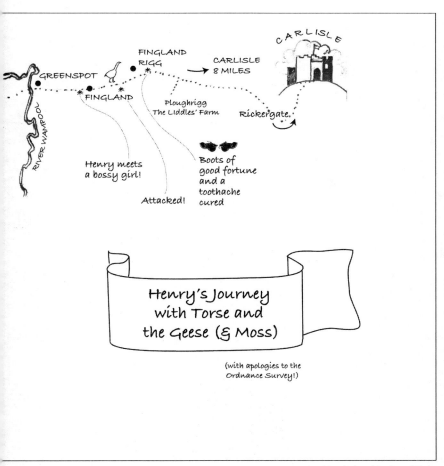

CARLISLE

FINGLAND
RIGG

CARLISLE
8 MILES

GREENSPOT

FINGLAND

Ploughrigg
The Liddles' Farm

Rickergate

RIVER WAMPOOL

Henry meets
a bossy girl!

Boots of
good fortune
and a
toothache
cured

Attacked!

Henry's Journey
with Torse and
the Geese (& Moss)

(with apologies to the
Ordnance Survey!)

Map designed by Anne Weeks

1

Leaving Home

The two figures hurried down the cobbled street to the docks. Nathan Gibbs, the man, surly in his stride, Henry, the boy, shivering as much from anxiety as from the chill night air.

Close by, Christ Church clock struck four, familiar, yet no longer the safe sound of yesterday.

Everything was happening so quickly. Nathan arguing with Henry's mother Elizabeth, bawling her out. Yelling he was tired of lines of washing forever cluttering the house, until suddenly he banged his fist down on the kitchen table and said Henry would start work now whether she liked it or not.

"He's still only thirteen," protested Elizabeth, white faced, her hands tightly clasped. "Have sense, man, he's too young!"

"He's a mouth too many! He'll earn his keep like anyone else!"

Upstairs Henry and Ruben huddled on their bed and could hear everything. Nathan's anger filled the brothers with dismay, their stepfather's anger, that is. Their real father had been dead now for four years.

Elizabeth was fraught, unsure, it was all too sudden. "What can he do at his age? He's still a child!"

"He'll go with the geese," said Nathan.

"He won't! Not with the drovers!"

"He's going, I tell you! I'll kick him out if I have to!" The row went on.

Ruben stared anxiously into the gloom. "Where's he going to send you?"

Henry shook his head. He didn't know. He tied a piece of string round his pants and grabbed a pullover.

"A long way . . . with the geese."

Ruben felt his chest constrict. Their bedroom felt unpleasant tonight and chilly.

"Not forever?"

"Course not!"

Ruben bit his lip. "What will Miss Dufton say? She'll send the inspector."

"Mum's to tell her I've run off."

"Who says?"

"*He* says. Now shut up."

Ruben paused uncertainly. "Can't I come too?"

"How can you? You're nobbut ten!"

Henry was shocked by the speed of it all.

Downstairs on the sideboard a family photograph in a silver frame was propped against a green teapot. The pot was a relic of better times and contained Elizabeth's hard earned washing money. Elizabeth stood with her two sons and a man, but the man was not Nathan. All four were unsmiling, holding their breath for the camera, the man whiskered and severe, Elizabeth, solemn eyed, a centre parting and not a hair out of place, both boys fair haired with intense stares ....

Henry, painfully thin yet somehow dependable looking, and Ruben, shoulders hunched from his weak chest.

In the scullery Elizabeth gave Henry a paper bag. It was still the middle of the night.

"Don't eat it all at once." She spoke softly, dreading his departure.

"I'll be all right, mum."

"Make sure you wash."

"I will."

"Behind your ears."

"Mum, I will!"

"Make sure you do!"

They clenched in an awkward hug. Nothing seemed real to Henry.

"You come straight home once you're through."

"I will," he promised. "Mum . . ." He paused anxiously, knowing this was his only chance.

"Mum . . . have I *got* to go?"

Her jaw tightened. "Your dad thinks it's best."

"He's not my dad," said Henry. Why didn't they remember?

"I just wish you'd try and get on better."

She looked at him ruefully. "Nay, who'll do all the repairs now?"

Handy Henry. No one called him that exactly, yet he had a certain knack for fixing things: the yard tap, a handle on the kettle, a new pothook over the fire.

"Ruben will help."

But he sounded unconvincing.

"Are you coming or have I got to drag you!" yelled Nathan.

"*Wait!*" Elizabeth snapped. "I'm getting him his food."

"They'll be unloading the boat and us not there!"

Upstairs, quickly now, Henry showed Ruben a small tin. It had a picture of a sailor on the lid holding a telescope. "It's for you. It's my most precious thing."

Ruben was open mouthed. He knew already what was inside.

"For me?"

"Don't you go and swap it!"

Ruben crossed his heart.

Inside the tin was a small satin Union flag. It was the most beautiful thing Ruben had ever seen and it had been given to Henry by the old seaman, Mr. Sharples, who lived next door when their dad was alive.

"I'll never let anyone have it," Ruben promised, his face bright.

Henry nodded, satisfied.

"Do I have to keep telling you?" yelled Nathan.

Henry hurried down filled with dread. He really was leaving.

They hugged and a moment later he was out in the street with Nathan.

"Henry, you take care," called Elizabeth.

She sounded forlorn.

The boy glanced back. His mother and Ruben were on the step. In the front window was a notice, unreadable in the half-light of a gas lamp but Henry knew well enough what it said: *Family washing done.*

From now on Ruben would have to collect the pram loads of dirty clothes by himself.

Boots for the Geese

Though it was still night, a corner of Silloth was wide awake. The little town, notched on the remote Cumberland coast, was hard at work earning its living. Noisy bellows and a blaze of acetylene lights greeted them as they turned in at the dock gates.

Henry had not been out this early before, but Nathan had.

He snapped: "I knew it! The *Yarrow's* here already!"

The steamer from Dublin lay alongside the quay alive with movement. Gates clanged as cows arrived on deck from the ship's belly and jostled down a ramp onto the quay. Yelling dockers whacked at the wilder beasts, hurrying them along into a cluster of pens. Yet the wildest beings were the drovers. Henry quickly recognised several – Dirty Dan, Old Potts, Shanks – and there were others around, Randy Dick, Big Arny, Brendan. All sailed across on the cattle runs each year, a rough cursing gang.

"Out of my way!" snarled Nathan, pushing through.

Mixed with the bellowing arose a secondary din.

Such a sight! A sea of brown and white met Henry's eyes. From fence to fence geese filled a long pen. Necks raised, the excited birds pushed and turned, cackling and honking. Intelligent, sharp eyes fastened on every movement of the hurrying dockers.

"And there is Torse himself!"

Nathan glared at Henry. "Be sure you let him think you know all about geese."

"But I don't . . . "

"None of your buts, you little devil! I've sent and told him you do!"

Nathan grabbed an ear and twisted hard.

"You'll do as I say or I'll thump ya!"

Tears stung the boy's eyes. But there was no chance to say anything. A ragged man engulfed in a shabby overcoat waded through the birds, his jaw bandaged. Henry recognised the drover. Two years ago he had sold them their Christmas goose.

He came straight up to them.

"Hah! So this is himself, is it?"

Henry found he was staring into a pair of wild eyes. The drover was small and round shouldered, almost buried in his coat. He did not look pleased.

"What's this? The whelp's a bag a bones!"

Nathan blustered. "Don't judge him by his size! He's a hard worker. You'll not find him wanting."

But the drover looked disgruntled. "With Liam not come, I need someone strong."

"The boy's strong."

"Liam is stronger."

"So why is he not here, then?"

"'Cause he's stupid! Coming with the geese, we are, as every year, and him gone to prison, thumping the constable in the gob."

The drover turned sharply. "Well? Do you know the road to the market, boy?"

Henry, surprised at the man's abruptness, coloured momentarily and seemed unable to speak. He caught sight of Nathan's face.

"No, mister, but I r–reckon it's not hard to f-find."

"Hah! So he can squawk! And have you helped with the geese afore?"

Henry, remembering Nathan's warning, nodded vigorously.

Torse's interest quickened. "Is that so? And where might that be?"

"A–at Christmas. When me mum and me was pushing it into the oven . . ."

The man's face darkened, then to Henry's surprise, despite the shabby bandage round his jaw he laughed.

"Well fancy that! A goose, into the oven!"

Nathan and Torse went off along the quay talking together, leaving Henry by the pen. Already it was growing light. He stared at the birds unenthusiastically. Irish geese just in from Dublin for fattening for Christmas. He remembered being attacked once by a vicious gander. It had pecked his neck and given him a bad fright. But he was smaller then. And now it seemed that he and this Torse man were going to set off together, though where to was unclear.

The men were not long away.

"All right, then, boy," said Torse. He gave Henry another hard stare. "Me and you are gonna walk 'um to market, and you'd better not let me down!"

"He'll not!" vowed Nathan. He glared at Henry to ensure he understood. Then: "A shilling?" he said to Torse.

"Ah, yes."

"A week?" Their glances met. The two men slapped their right hands, palm to palm. Henry's fate had been decided.

"Make sure you bring your pay home," warned Nathan. He seemed about to say more but a tall figure was approaching.

Torse groaned. "Just what I don't need. It's that misery of a vet."

"Then I'll be away," said Nathan.

As Henry watched him go he felt a moment's panic. Even Nathan was better than going with this wild drover.

"So who's this?" demanded the tall newcomer.

The vet was wiry, dressed in black, his face creased with long wrinkles. Henry thought he looked like an undertaker.

A servile expression came over the drover. His voice changed from its roughness to something gentler. A note of cringe crept in.

"Your royal honour, bless us! Tis me new helper on the road."

"Taking on shrimps are we? And who's given you a beating?"

"Not a beating, your honour, but the toothache. A wicked toothache plaguing me day and night, destroying me holy prayers."

Swiftly the drover turned to Henry. "Help him, boy! Don't just stand staring!"

Hurriedly Henry dragged open the gate into the pen and immediately the vet began dipping down among the geese, grabbing and examining their feet. He was very quick. Torse followed, clutching at his jaw. "All good birds," enthused the drover. "Never had better!"

They waded back and forth and eventually the vet came

out. In his hands was a goose, hissing fiercely.

"Broken foot."

The drover peered at the bird in disbelief. Sure enough, one of its feet hung loosely.

"It can't walk," said the vet.

"Your honour, that I never saw. Would you believe it!"

"Lucky for you it's just the one. I'll pass the rest."

"Then your honour is a gentleman."

The vet loomed over the drover.

"I'll take care of the injured goose, your honour . . ."

But the vet held on to the bird. "I'll see personally that it is destroyed in accordance with gov'ment regulations."

The men's eyes met.

"You be right," said the drover unconvincingly.

The vet went off to examine a pen of cattle, the goose crooked under an arm.

"Regulations!" muttered the drover. "Stew pot regulations! A wicked thief he is, stealing a poor man's goose!"

And then to Henry: "Don't stare, boy. There's work to be done. You *can* work can you?"

Henry flushed red. "Of course I can . . . "

"Then get started! Do you know what we do first? No? What *do* you know, eh? Nothing, I dare say! Then listen: you and me's going to give these geese the finest boots they's ever had, or they'll not walk a mile. You stay close – and when I say jump, you jump!"

Uncertainty overcame Henry. Jump? Where was he supposed to jump? He waited to find out.

The drover hurried to the dock wall and seized what Henry thought was a wooden trough, except it had no ends. "Don't stand looking useless, get a hold!"

Man and boy dragged it across to the geese pen.

"This is called a *raise*, see? Special for the job. Now get the other!"

A second trough was lined up to the first, end-to-end, forming a long passage two feet wide. Torse thrust a giant shovel into Henry's hands.

"Hold that! I'll be back."

Along the quay a brazier was glowing red with coals. A bucket of tar lumps stood waiting pungent, melted, ready for use. The drover staggered up with it and tipped a hot liquid stream into the raise. As he did so something tumbled out of his coat and clattered to the quay.

Without meaning to, Henry reached it first. It was a black knobbly stick, a kind of club, shiny with handling. Small hands though he had, one end of it fitted comfortably within his palm.

"What is it?"

Torse snatched it away. "You leave that alone, boy!"

His voice was sharp. Henry stared in surprise.

"That's me shillelagh. Good Irish oak. Nothing bad happens to us, see, not while I have me shillelagh! Now get to the geese."

Cackling broke out as the smell of the tar reached the birds.

"Shovel the sand down," Torse ordered.

But Henry got it wrong.

"No, no, no! Not in the *tar,* you eejit, in the other one. That's it! Now I'll be sending the geese through, and you keep plenty of sand for 'em to walk on! Do you think you can do that!"

"I knows what to do," said Henry suddenly angry. The man was making him sound stupid. Well, he'd show him!

The shovel was a brute, heavy and rusty. Henry struggled,

scattering sand in the passage where Torse had ordered. As he did so the drover opened the pen.

His voice took on a coaxing tone. "Come on, me pretties! Come on!"

Cackling broke out as he wafted his shillelagh.

"Come along! Lovely boots this way!"

Henry joined in until several birds paused uncertainly at the edge of the tar.

"Jipe! Jipe! Jipe!" shouted Torse.

More geese pressed in from behind and suddenly the leading birds paddled through the black puddle. Not liking the stickiness, they hurried on across Henry's heap of sand.

"That's it! Keep 'em going!"

The geese began to move through in a growing rush. As fast as the tar was used up, Torse poured more in their path and Henry shovelled sand till his arms felt they were breaking.

They brought more sand, and there was not enough tar. More had to be melted over the brazier. It took time and Torse swore impatiently. In a flurry one of the wilder geese escaped. Henry chased it down the dockside and drove it back.

Later in the afternoon Nathan returned. "You've done then?"

Drover and boy sat on the ground worn out.

"Done," said Torse. "Six hundred, all done."

The geese were back inside their pen. Each one had been shod with tough pads of sand and tar.

"And the boy?"

"Sure, he is terrible slow, but I'm learnin' him."

Nathan seized Henry and towed him out of the hearing of the drover. "You work hard or you'll get a belting!"

"I will," protested Henry. "I am."

"Make sure you do."

Henry caught a whiff of beer.

"And don't lose your pay, or I'll tan your bum red."

Nathan released hold and Henry turned back towards the geese, a cold patch within him.

Everywhere in the pen birds were lifting up their padded feet, getting used to the extra weight.

Torse stared into Henry's face but said nothing. Henry disliked him too.

3

In the Doss

The drover made sure the pen gate was secure, and then for the first time since Henry had met him the man's shoulders relaxed.

"And what's it with you, then?"

His voice was less harsh now. The pressure to finish the tarring was over.

Henry, startled, looked blank.

"What's your name? You've got a name, have you?"

"It's Henry . . . Hodgekin."

"Henry Hodkin, eh!"

"Hodge-kin."

"That's not your father's name"

"He's not me real dad."

Torse eyed the boy's bare feet. His toes were straight and tanned.

"Have you no boots?"

Henry shook his head. Why did everyone stare? Lots of boys had bare feet.

"The road'll be wicked with stones. You need boots."

"I doesn't. I don't need none."

"Is that so?" The man's stare grew more intent. "Afore we've done, you'll wish you'd trod in the tar, same as the geese."

"I'll be all right," said Henry stubbornly.

The drover chewed on a sliver of tobacco but left the matter at that. To Torse the boy was cheap labour.

Almost timidly, Henry asked: "Can – can I go home now?"

The man stared, surprised. "Home? Who said annything 'bout home?"

"I – I just . . ."

"You stop with me now, boy, till the job's done. Home! We've a long walk with the geese before there'll be anny sign of home!"

Tarring the geese had taken most of the day. Evening was on them and the streets of the little town were beginning to empty. Beyond the giant shed stood a warehouse where a wooden shack sagged against its walls. Torse headed for it.

"Never bin in here afore, have you? No! Well, 'tis the Doss."

Henry knew about the Doss, every boy and girl in town did, but none went inside. Parents warned them to keep away.

The drover pushed in and Henry was surprised to find the place was already full of men. It was oven-hot and reeked of sweat and dung.

"Hah!"

Faces turned their way.

"'Tis Torse the Goose."

Light from a paraffin lantern lit up the drovers. They were a rough looking bunch. A few huddled round an iron stove, but most sprawled on sacking.

"Who's let that young beggar in?"

A black haired man glared at Henry. It was Shanks.

Another man smiled.

"Oh, he's a darling, let him stay!" He clutched at one of Henry's legs.

Henry shrank back.

"Keep your filthy self to yourself," chimed Torse angrily. "The boy's with me."

"And where's that weasel brother of yours?" said Shanks.

"Me brother's broken his leg, he has, and this is who's walking the geese with me to Carlisle."

Henry stared at Torse. So they were going to Carlisle. And Liam, broken his leg now! Last time Torse had said his brother had gone to jail, but perhaps both were true.

The drover pushed the boy down against a wall. "Got grub has you?"

"I's got me bait."

"Bait? What bait? Fishing are you?"

Henry tugged the packet out of his jacket.

"It's what we call it," he said defensively. He found a pasty inside the paper bag, along with bread and cheese.

"Aye, well, don't you be moving till I give the word! And give that me!"

The drover snatched away the bread and cheese. "We shares everything, see!"

No one interfered. The boy was Torse's concern. The drover retreated into the group round the stove and broke up the bread, storing half within his coat and starting on the rest himself.

"So, you're a-droving?"

Henry found himself beside a man with a bright face. His hair was as wild as any of them, but he was younger, perhaps in his twenties. Another drover.

"Aye, mister. We got six hundred geese."

"Six hundred!"

The pasty had become badly mashed and Henry carefully separated the bits from the paper.

"That's a good lot of geese to look after."

Henry did not know whether it was or was not. He was starving and started on the pasty.

"And what might that be, when you are at home?"

Henry gulped down a chunk. "It's a fiddle pasty." He quoted his mother: "*Summat fiddled out of nowt.*"

The man grinned. Then he eyed Torse where a bottle of spirit was beginning to go the rounds.

"Just how much would a young fella like you be being paid, I mean, you walking all the way to Carlisle?"

Henry hesitated. He did not know this stranger.

"No, no, don't split if you isn't wanting."

"A shilling," confided Henry. And, in a quieter voice: "A week."

"A whole shilling!" The other nodded approvingly. It was good pay for a boy. The drover stared at Torse. "Let me give you some advice. Be sure once you's in Carlisle he pays you, or he'll diddle you, he will."

"My mum will bash him if he don't."

"He'll diddle her, too, given the chance."

Henry looked solemn faced. "Are you walking the geese?"

"Not me! I'm a cattle walloper! Geese is too slow for me. But don't you try cattle. Kick your bum they do when you isn't looking! You stick with the geese."

The bottle landed their way and the drover supped a long hard gullet full and handed it over.

Henry looked worried. "I never has . . ."

"Then now's your chance."

Torse turned his head sharply from the stove. "Don't be wasting that on the boy!"

"You sup away," urged the young drover.

Burning fire poured down Henry's throat. His anguished gasp filled the hut with laughter.

"You's a drover now, lad!"

"Sup again!"

"Put hairs on your chest, that will!"

Henry pushed the bottle from him, still gasping.

The young drover grinned.

"Kills nasty germs, it does!" His voice dropped. "Mind what I told you. You watch Torse. Bin in jail he has, pinching. He'll diddle you."

Henry sank against the wall, listening to the talk. He was feeling homesick. In his home town, yet he was homesick.

The door opened to let in another drover. A wild thought overcame him: he must escape! Run away. But where could he go? He daren't go back home, not with Nathan there. The man would kick him out again.

Henry remembered Monday. He and Ruben had brought home a stray dog off the beach. They had got it a lump of bread out of the bread tin and Nathan had been furious.

"No damn dog's stopping in this house! Not while I'm here, it isn't!"

"It's a sheepdog," Henry cried. "It's hungry."

Savagely Nathan had grabbed the dog by its scruff and had thrown it out into the back lane.

"He was doing no harm!" yelled Henry.

A stinging blow sent him reeling into the dresser.

"Another word from you and you'll get more than that!"

Upstairs Henry had wept into his pillow. Nothing was

ever right any more. But the matter of the dog was not over. Next morning when the boys went to school the dog was lying outside the yard gate, its head flat to the ground.

Acting quickly, Henry grabbed the creature and pushed it down among the bags of washing in the outshed. There might be a chance.

An anxious day followed. At four o'clock they raced home but the dog had gone. They searched the outshed; they searched the house. They searched the streets.

Down on the shore Henry met Robin Jackson from Form B. He said he had seen Nathan dragging the dog to the harbour. Henry raced to the docks and searched every corner, but there was no sign of the dog. He stared into the water. Nathan would have drowned it. He knew he would.

The Doss grew hotter and he curled up on the sacking. He wondered if his mother and Ruben were still awake. By the time the bottle of spirit came round again he was asleep.

4

On the Road

Henry followed Torse along the quay. Almost four o'clock and his clothes felt too thin in the night air. It seemed only moments ago that a noisy game of cards was taking place in the Doss. Only moments, yet the place was full of heavy breathing and snores when the drover woke him with a prod of his boot and towed him into the cold.

Together they reached the line of pens.

"Geese be slower than cattle," said Torse. He spoke in a low voice so it did not carry. "We've got to be clear of the bullock wallopers afore they get going."

"W-where are they going?" said Henry.

"Same place as us."

He prodded a grubby finger down on Henry's shoulder.

"Your job's to keep the geese moving steady. But quiet. Nice and quiet! If you start 'em quiet they stays quiet."

Henry only half listened. He was shivering with the cold. Urged on by the drover, he got into the pen and began to slap his arms round his body. "Get on, with you!" he called.

A wave of cackling erupted.

"Jaysus, boy, are you stupid!" hissed Torse angrily. "Don't

you listen? I said quiet!"

The honking grew louder.

"Here you silly eejit! Use this!"

The man thrust a puffy object over the railings. Henry had seen one once before. It was a pig's bladder, blown up like a balloon on a string. It had a long stick for a handle, a bit like a whip, only gentler.

"Tap 'em with that! Now get 'em moving!"

But the damage was done. The geese were roused and a noisy protest erupted as Henry started to waft the bladder to and fro. Except for the noise nothing seemed to happen, then reluctantly the flock started to edge out through the gateway.

Too slowly for the drover.

"Tap 'em, boy! Tap 'em. Don't just stand peeing yourself."

"I know what to do," said Henry, annoyed.

"Oh, you know do you! Think you're clever, eh?"

Henry glared and hurried about the pen, urging the geese forward. He was fed up with the drover. He should have stayed awake and escaped. Well he would, the next chance he got he would go.

The birds padded out into the open and started to move down the quay. Slowly they left the docks.

They reached a web of railway lines at the level crossings and the flock moved over in a disgruntled wave, not enjoying the shiny rails.

Henry tried to steer them towards the road that led out of town.

At once a flotilla headed off in a contrary direction.

"Stop 'em, boy. Stop 'em!"

Henry set off at a run. The birds swerved, the wrong way. How could these slow things suddenly go so fast! He got to the front and spread his arms. Crikey! Wrong way again.

"Get back!" he yelled. He raced to and fro, knowing he was doing badly and just as he thought it would never go right the rebels turned and rejoined the flock and were back on course.

Henry was left gasping.

Torse looked angry. "You gotta do better than that, boy! When we turn off the road you gotta be in front and see they go the right way. And when you are not there, you gotta be back here alongside me, and keep the divils going straight. You got that?"

Henry nodded.

At last they passed the final house. Henry was relieved and slowed down but Torse exclaimed in annoyance. "Don't stop, now, boy! They'll get at the grass edges."

That seemed odd. "What's wrong with that?"

"Jaysus! Don't you know anything? They's famished, see."

The man waved his arms. "They'll stop anywhere if there's grass to feed on! Keep 'um going till we're clear of the wallopers. Now get on with it!"

Henry was angry. Nothing he did was right! Worse, he was hungry and wished he was back at home. Every step was taking him further away. He had been this far in the past with Ruben, but from here on the road ahead was unknown. He knew that Carlisle was a long way, and what would happen when he got there? He had never been to Carlisle.

The geese soon required all his attention. Constant watching was needed to keep them off the verges. As the sun rose he began to feel less chilled. The road twisted across the Solway plateau through a low-lying marshy world. Slow-moving, billowing clouds rolled high overhead. Under this great morning sky Henry's goose trek started, though what lay ahead he could not even guess. Nor at this moment did he realise that they were not alone. Far behind them a shadowy creature was moving in their wake, a dog, nervous, unsure, holding back.

An uneasy hour passed and something was wrong. Twice Torse stopped in the track to listen, his head tilted. "Do you hear anything, boy?"

Henry was fed up and suddenly didn't care what he said.

"Aye, the geese is making a row."

Torse scowled peevishly.

"Oh, are they! Well we don't want no wallopers! Not before we get to our own bit of road – and less of your lip!"

"What's our bit?"

"Where there's no wallopers. Now get moving."

Henry tried hard but the flock seemed to trail along more slowly than before and this sad state lasted until the road widened into broad grass verges. Contrarily the birds started to rush forward.

"No, no! Keep 'em off!" yelled the drover.

Henry was already hurrying to get round the leading birds. Back and forth he raced till he was out of breath. Slowly he got the geese moving again.

Torse stood watching. "You've gotta watch geese better than that. They'll go and fool you."

Henry paid little attention. When the right moment came he would run away. He had had enough of the drover; he had had enough of the geese.

Torse however had other ideas.

"You ever caught a goose, boy?"

Henry glared. "No. And I don't want to!"

"Oh, don't you! Well you're gonna learn!"

He waved his shillelagh at the tail end of the flock. "Get hold on that little one. And don't be scared of it."

Henry eyed the goose warily.

"I isn't scared!"

He flushed, knowing he was a bit.

"Then *do* it!" said the drover.

The goose certainly was little, but Henry knew that geese had strong wings and could hurt. He spread his arms.

"Get it away from the others."

Henry closed in, pretending he knew what he was doing. The goose watched him coming, then in a rush it set off towards the hedge.

Torse spluttered. "Don't just *fan* it, you eejit! Get hold!"

"I am! I am!"

Henry lunged at the bird but missed. A stinging blow from a wing lashed him on his nose.

"Hah!" snorted the disgusted drover. "I teld you, I teld you!"

Blood ran down Henry's face.

"That's what comes of having a big nose!"

"My nose is *not* big!" said Henry angrily. It wasn't. He knew it wasn't.

"Watch me, boy! Watch me!"

The man closed in on another bird. A moment later it was clamped under the drover's right arm. His speed came as a surprise. Despite everything, Henry was impressed.

"Next time be quicker!"

They moved off again and for a while made good progress, but it did not last.

"What is it?" asked Henry.

For the third time in minutes the drover was staring back along the road.

"Nothing, boy. Keep the birds moving!" he ordered.

"I am! It's not me who keeps stopping."

Twice more Torse paused to stare behind him, and then the flock reached a narrow sidetrack. It twisted away through low-lying fields, little better than a cart track with grass growing down the middle but Torse looked pleased.

"This is it. Down this way, boy!"

Taking his time Henry turned the leading birds into it and the rest followed.

"Good. We're doing good! We'll see no cattle now! They'll take the other way, they will."

Henry was scarcely interested. He was famished. If the geese had walked a stony mile and a half, he felt he had done ten. He looked up at the sun and was surprised. Already it had gone dinnertime. It was desperately slow work.

The flock reached another lush verge and this time Torse let them graze. Man and boy flopped to the ground.

The drover began a muttering rummage inside his coat and produced a bundle. He unwrapped a hunk of bread.

Henry's smouldering glare met him.

"And what are you looking at? You and your nose."

Shiftily the drover tore a piece off the bread and stuffed it into his mouth. "You've got my bait," said Henry indignantly. "That's my grub, what you pinched!"

"Ohhhhh, is that so!" The drover scowled. "Pinched it, have I! That's a nasty thought to be finding in a young boy!"

But Henry persisted. "My mum gave that grub to me."

"Hah! Did she, now! And I was thinking she gave it the both of us!"

Henry scowled. Without thinking, he grabbed at the

remaining bread. As if by magic the man's shillelagh came out from under his coat. It cracked across Henry's knuckles.

"Don't you get wild with me, boy! Or things will start hurting, so they will!"

Henry stared angrily, his eyes stung to tears. "You're a thief," he yelled. He waved his throbbing fingers.

"Hah!"

"And a liar! " He jumped to his feet. "And ya can walk the geese yourself!"

Any earlier timidity Henry had ever felt vanished. He felt a wave of triumph. He had told him! The thought had come unexpectedly and now it was out!

Torse paused surprised and stared nastily. "So *that's* it! You would be running away would you!"

A stench of vile breath, then two hard eyes swam into Henry's vision as the drover dragged him up to his grizzled face. "Take one wrong step, and I'll have the garda after you, I will! You got that!"

He thrust Henry from him.

Henry was both furious and wary – the man's shillelagh was not to be ignored.

Torse turned his back and sat muttering into his coat. Even so, he knew there was sense in keeping up the boy's strength. He broke a piece off the loaf, tossing it over.

"Don't say I haven't given you your share, you ungrateful divil! Now eat up. Tomorrow I'll learn you how we eats proper."

Henry tore it to pieces. He was ravenous. Until this moment he had not thought how he was going to find food on the long road to Carlisle. Given a maggot butty and right now he would have eaten it.

Still chewing, he examined Torse more closely. The

drover was shabby, his hair wild, his boots a-glitter with nails. And he smelt! What was strange was his coat. It seemed to be layers deep and almost down to the ground. The drover had unbuttoned it against the day's growing heat and Henry was surprised to see that the man inside was quite small.

More than anything Henry wanted to get away. But how could he go home without money? His mother needed anything he could earn. In any case, he was supposed to give his wages to Nathan. Two shillings, if he got them. A patch of hopelessness formed within him. The last thing he wanted was to give it to Nathan.

A groan made him turn. Torse had risen and was standing stiff and tense.

"What's up?" said Henry.

"Listen, boy! Are you deaf?"

No answer was needed. Back along the track a bellow of cattle sounded. A hurrying mass of heads raced into sight.

"The geese!" yelled Torse. "Move the geese!"

Henry tried, but there was no chance of success.

The leading beasts charged towards the flock. For a moment the leaders faltered, wide-eyed and snorting, then they plunged through.

Pandemonium! A sea of terrified birds shrieked into the air.

Two men raced along behind the cattle, beating at them with long sticks.

"Jipe! Jipe! Jipe!" Their yells filled the afternoon. Fierce grins! Flashes of triumph! Henry recognised them from the Doss, rough and unshaven. Cattle wallopers!

The rampage lasted moments, yet the effect was devastating. Of the six hundred birds, more than a quarter fought their way through the hedges into the meadows.

Henry gaped, at a loss what to do.

"Jaysus, boy! What ails ya?" yelled the drover. "Get after 'em!"

Henry rushed forward and in his haste stumbled on something spongy. It went off with a bang! He scrambled into the nearest field as Torse danced up and down waving his stick at the receding cattle. The code was unwritten, but it was well enough known among the drovers – wherever the roads allowed, cattlemen and geese men kept to their own separate ways. It had been so for generations. Today the code had been broken.

"I'll murder you, Shanks!" yelled the drover. "I'll murder you, I will!"

It took them a frustrating half-hour to round up the scattered birds and get them back into the main flock. Henry retied the string round his pants, and threw the remains of the bladder over a hedge.

5

Dawn Wallops

Henry was in agony but he was too embarrassed to say so. It was late evening already with every goose on the track foot weary and Torse anxious to find a halt for the night. It was not easy, for there was a risk involved.

"We need a good little field," he told Henry, then seeing the boy's face: "And what the divil's the matter with you?"

Henry wriggled up and down and looked desperate. "I want the lav."

"Oh, do you! Well you can wait till we've settled the geese."

But no, that wouldn't do.

"I can't. It's now."

"Messed your pants, have you!"

Henry was indignant. "No, I haven't!"

"Serve you right if you have."

"I haven't!"

"Well get behind the hedge!"

Henry hesitated.

"And what's the matter now?"

"I've no paper."

"Paper! God bless us, 'tis Her Majesty herself! Use a fist of grass like the rest of us!"

Henry scrambled through a hedge, burning with shame. Even at home the nettie had squares of newspaper tied up on a piece of string. His dislike for the drover grew.

The frustrating search for somewhere to stop for the night went on. They came to a gate bound up with wire. A second gate had rocks piled against it. Farmers were wary of passing drovers.

At last, ignoring Torse, Henry went ahead on his own. He was tired and fed up. He didn't know if his luck would be any better than the drover's but he couldn't do worse. Two fields later he discovered a paddock with an unlocked gate.

Torse had a look for himself. "It'll do, get 'em in! But keep 'em quiet, boy. This time no shouting, see! We'll get away sharp at first light afore anyone sees us!"

Henry did not like the sound of that.

"What if the farmer comes?"

"He won't! But if one does, you leave him to me. I know how to deal with farmers. Now take this and fetch water for a brew."

He thrust a tin into Henry's hand.

Henry stared, baffled.

"Water? What water?"

The drover sighed in exasperation.

"How do I know what water? Find a spring! Look in the hedges."

Henry nearly flung the tin onto the grass. Orders, orders, orders! He was fed up with the man. But the drover had turned to the flock and was checking for any injured birds.

Footsore, Henry returned to the little road and set off along the hedgerows. Water! He had seen no water all day.

The man was impossible.

He went almost a mile and he was telling himself yet again that he was never going to find any when he discovered a horse trough set in the hedge. The water tasted good. Pleased, he hurried back with the tin brimming.

Torse had lit a fire and had spread his coat on the ground. Henry saw now why it was so big. The man had jacked up the collar end with a stick from the hedge, turning it into a tent-like den.

"I teld you there'd be water!" The drover sat by the fire looking smug. "Now we'll have a brew."

The tea was scalding but good. Henry got the lid; Torse got the tin. But if the tea helped there was little to eat. The drover divided up the last of Henry's loaf, keeping the bigger piece for himself. Henry noticed but he said nothing, searching for every crumb where they had fallen.

Night was almost on them. Henry paused uncertainly in the gloom. Where was he going to sleep?

"Well, don't just stand there," snapped the drover. "Settle yourself in the ditch and get some rest. It'll be daylight soon enough."

Henry's mouth opened in protest. "A ditch! I've never slept in a ditch."

"Hah! Then now's your chance to learn. You'll be soaked with dew if you stand in the open."

Muttering at the foolishness of the world, the drover shuffled backwards into his den.

Henry groaned. He felt about with a hand at the bottom of the nearest ditch and was surprised to find it was dry. Holding his breath, he sank into its depths only to sit up again in a panic as grass closed over his head. He paused, deeply unhappy. Already there were stars in the sky but for some reason they made him shiver. It was all right for Torse in his coat. Henry had never realised how thin his own clothes were. He lay back down and a long struggle took place in the dark while he scraped together a wodge of dry grass for a pillow. It wasn't very comfortable but it would do. Close by, the geese were chattering softly. He listened and wondered what they were saying. They hadn't been all that bad to keep going, not really, though there were a lot of them. Still he wanted to get away and given a chance, he would.

Slowly the moon rose. A current of air flowed across the paddock and with it came a pleasant smell of leaves . . .

Without intending anything of the sort Henry fell asleep. He never stirred as Torse got up under the stars and went round the flock to make sure the birds were all right; he never heard the drover's occasional groans as the man's tooth troubled him. The first thing he knew was when something began to creep down into the dike and a hairy body brushed against his face.

Henry let out a gasp of fright.

"Get away!" he yelled, jerking upright. And then he paused, not believing his senses. Even in the dark he realised what it was.

It was the sheepdog.

The dog gave a low whine and immediately Henry wished he had not eaten all his bread. Despite his yell Torse was still asleep. What would he say when he woke? Come morning he would find out for sure. But how had the dog found him? Henry was amazed. It was shivering and he brought it down alongside him. They could keep each other warm. The dog's sudden appearance had another effect, a good one, for the first time since setting out Henry felt happier. Still marvelling, he fell asleep and the night moved on.

But it did not remain peaceful.

Shouting filled the paddock. Henry woke to find that it was dawn and a farmer was beating Torse furiously with a stick.

"Help! Your honour! Stop! I can explain!" yelled the drover. "Ouch! Ow! Stop!"

"Sneak your geese into my field, would you!" bellowed the farmer. "Take that, you varmint!"

Somehow the drover struggled clear and the blow missed.

Torse, however, did not stop yelling. "Your honour, you was asleep when we arrived! We was going to pay you at first light! On my honour we was!"

The farmer seemed to be twice the size of the drover, a bullnecked man with a big tanned face. He had had enough of passing geese fouling the grass.

"Get out!" he bellowed.

"At once, your honour! At once!" The drover waved frantically at Henry who was sitting in the ditch petrified. "Get up you eejit! The gentleman wants his field cleared!"

The farmer swivelled. "So! Two of you is there! *And* a dog! Well you can begger off, the lot of you, before I get the constable!"

"A dog?" Torse stared wild-eyed at the ditch, but there was no time to explain. In a panic Henry and Torse scrambled to round up the geese. Under the farmer's glare, they drove them towards the gate and only by chance did the flock find the gap at the first attempt. The birds poured through, Henry hot and bothered urging them on. Even so it seemed to take an age.

But it was not over. Some farmers took what money they

could get but others preferred a good fight. As Torse grabbed up his coat, the man lunged and almost lifted him off the ground. Terrified, the drover awaited a first punch.

But it was money.

"That'll cost you sixpence!" demanded the man. "For the night's stay."

"Oh, your honour, yes! Most generous," gasped the drover. He struggled a hand into a pocket. "Sixpence! I have the very one here, your honour, if you'll be letting me down now!"

The coin was snatched away.

"And a goose," said the farmer, not letting go.

"Your honour?"

"A good fat one."

The man's grip tightened.

Torse, greatly alarmed, struggled madly and broke free.

"A goose, boy! Get the man a goose!"

Henry acted quickly. He drove the nearest bird forward and Torse snatched it up."A beauty, your honour. The very best!"

Fearing that still more expensive demands might follow, he rammed the bird into the farmer's arms. The bird was as shocked as the man. It hissed bad temperedly and began pecking furiously at everything in sight.

Any other time Henry would almost have laughed as the farmer fought to hold the bird, but now he found himself left with the entire flock. Torse was legging it away along the track leaving Henry to get the geese moving again.

It was an inglorious exit.

6

A Free Feed

"We don't want no dog with us!" yelled Torse.

"Well he's coming!" Henry yelled back.

"He'll frighten the birds."

"No he won't!" Exasperated, Henry pointed at the dog.

"Look at him!" The dog was lying at the roadside flat to the ground, his eyes fixed on the flock in deep concentration, unmoving, willing them not to pass him.

"He's not frightening 'em! He's guarding 'em like he would if they was sheep. You can see he is."

"Nonsense!"

"He'll be a good help," said Henry defiantly. "I'm keeping him. And he's called Moss."

"Moss? How'd you know he's called Moss?"

"Cause that's a proper Cumberland sheepdog name."

"Pah!"

They had halted half a mile along the road. The geese were attacking the verges. Man and boy were tired and hungry and to make matters worse Torse's toothache was not improving. His bandage had disappeared in the tussle.

"Well I'm not saying yes," said the drover, tearing a strip of lining out of his coat. "Now fix me a new bandage."

"You said you knew how to deal with farmers," said Henry accusingly.

Torse glared. "And so I did, didn't I? Paid him a good sixpence for the night's stay! And did he not get the fine gift of a goose to fatten for Christmas? Now tie this on and stop your nonsense."

Henry knew this was not the truth of the matter. He struggled with the rag. Drawing the two ends together he tied them in a bow on the top of the drover's head. "I've done you a bow," he told him.

"No, no, it wants a knot!" Torse protested. He huddled on the ground fingering his jaw. "A bow's no good. A bow'll come undone, so it will!"

"All right, all right."

Henry pulled impatiently at the two ends and undid the bow. He tied it more carefully but it still ended up looking like a bow.

"That's too tight, you eejit!"

"Do you want me to do it or don't you?" said Henry exasperatedly.

The drover muttered and squirmed.

"You're making it slip," Henry warned.

"Just fix it!"

They got the flock moving again. Moss seemed to know exactly what to do, padding to and fro in their wake helping to keep the stragglers going. It was as if he had done it many times.

"He must have been a proper sheepdog," said Henry. "You can tell."

"Well sheep isn't geese," snapped Torse, but privately he

knew that some drovers did use sheepdogs to drive their geese. Not that he was going to tell Henry.

They reached a small junction and Torse stopped in the track and lifted a hand.

"Now then. *Yes!*" he exclaimed.

Henry groaned. What now?

The drover's body had grown very quiet. He moved forward peering into the rankness of the nearest hedge. The geese were milling around, seemingly forgotten. It was an old beautiful hedge, untrimmed, spilling profusely over the verge. Henry could see nothing special about it and he followed, puzzled. What was the man up to?

Outside a cottage the drover halted.

"A-ha!" His bandaged face eased fractionally. "The very one! Now, boy, pay attention. It's your next lesson. And mark every word I says, 'cause your turn will be next."

Henry rolled his eyes. Orders. Always orders!

A dumpy woman opened the cottage door.

In an amazing transformation, an air of gentle humility came over the drover. From a wild looking man armed with a dangerous looking stick, he turned into a humble goose walker badly in need of sympathy and help along the hard road of life, the ever-hard road. As the woman stared inquiringly, the drover ducked his head and touched a finger to his forehead.

"Good day to you, missis." His voice had become engaging and warm. "We're on the road to market, we are, and sadly hungry, and I've got me frail young friend here starving and hardly able to walk for want of food, and wondering we was if you'd be sparing us a brew of nourishing tea to lift our weary spirits?"

The woman's gaze settled first on the bow on top of the

drover's head, and then on to Henry himself, at which she smiled warmly.

"And how long have you been on the road, young man?"

Henry was startled, not having expected to be addressed.

"Tell her, boy, tell her!"

"Since yesterday morning," said Henry. "From Silloth."

"Oh, deary me, then you must be hungry," said the little woman kindly.

"He is, he is!" agreed Torse. "Very hungry he is, missis, not having eaten more than a morsel in the whole of a day and a night, and that given by me own humble self to the poor living lamb!"

Henry stared in surprise at Torse's outburst, but he remained silent as the woman bade them wait.

And soon the two drovers were sitting in the shade of a tree watching over the geese and eating better than for many a long hour. A free feed! Bread and cheese, Slab biscuit and a can of sweet hot tea passed between them. Despite a glare from Torse, Henry broke his biscuit in half and fed it to Moss.

The spirits of the two drovers began to improve, and Torse with an eye to Henry's appealing face, made him take back the empty tin to offer their thanks. It worked and Henry was rewarded with several more biscuits.

"God bless you, missis," broke in the humble drover edging forward to see what had happened; and then, as if he had said it often in the past, he added in a special voice:

"Tis a Godly house you keep, and we thank you for it."

"Aye, well, that's as maybe," said their benefactress. She eyed Henry's skinny legs. "Just you keep this young lad properly fed. He's a sight too thin, he is."

Torse bobbed in acknowledgement. "Oh I will, missis, I

will. I couldn't treat him better than if he was me own darling son."

And with this lying remark, once round the first corner he snatched the biscuits off Henry and stuffed them inside his coat.

"And none of your complaints!" Torse warned.

"Of course not," Henry told him innocently.

"Now give me the rest!" snapped the drover.

Henry was startled.

"I haven't got none."

The man grabbed his arm threateningly. "Give 'em now or I'll shake them out of you!"

Henry protested. "She gave 'em to me, not you!"

But he saw that Torse knew and he fished out the biggest piece of biscuit from his trouser pocket. In doing this he managed to leave a few of the bits for Moss. The drover had won this time, but he wouldn't if it happened again. Next time Henry would be ready for him. He knew exactly how he would get his revenge.

7

Crooked Dealing

The woman's note of criticism had registered, though not about food. Torse turned his fierce eyes on Henry. "Now, boy, I've been thinking, it's time you was learning something useful if you're to be a real drover."

They had reached a low wooded hill. A signpost pointed along a pleasant leafy lane towards Abbeytown.

"But I don't want to be a drover," Henry protested.

"Oh! You don't! Then Jaysus, boy, what are you doing now if you ain't a-droving?"

Henry felt caught out. He blurted the only thing he could think of, how it would help his mother. It was the money . . .

"Ah!" Torse held up a hand. Money he understood. "Then it's time for a lesson. Torse the Goose will learn you how to sell geese!"

Henry groaned. "I don't want to sell geese! I want to go home!"

The drover glared. "You'll go home when I says! Now get the geese moving and listen hard when I shows ya."

A quarter of an hour later they reached a farm. Leaving

the geese in the road Torse and Henry entered a cobbled yard. Unexpectedly Torse called out loudly: "Why, good day, to you, your honour."

The drover's voice had changed. It had become warm and cheerful. It took Henry by surprise. The man almost sounded important. He even seemed to stand a little taller.

A farmer was backing out of a barn doorway wheeling a barrow load of muck.

Torse propelled Henry well to the front so that his thinness could be appreciated. "Me hungry young friend and me is walking the geese to Carlisle," he declared. "We wonder if your honour would be wanting a few good Irish birds to fatten for Christmas?"

The man came over bringing a ripe smell of cow muck with him. He stared into the road where the flock had settled. "Oh, aye?"

He did not seem over eager, but Torse knew all about canny Cumbrians and was not put off.

"Little 'uns, is they?"

"But good!" enthused Torse. "Good Christmas fatteners, and cheap."

The farmer's face grew a shade shrewder. "And how cheap might that be?"

"Very, your honour. But look for yourself."

The man went out and took his time.

"Lovely birds, your honour."

"Aye, there seems ta be some good uns among 'em, a bit scraggy with it. All right, I might chance a few if the price is right."

"Not even two shillings, your honour, to you just one shilling . . . and a sixpence."

The man's face turned bleak.

"One and threepence," said Torse quickly.

Henry guessed what the man was really thinking.

"Make 'em a shilling a-piece," said the farmer, "and I'll have fifty."

He gave a tight smile.

Henry smirked.

Torse groaned.

"Your honour, I would be giving them away!"

"A shilling," said the man. "And I chooses me own."

"Of course, your honour. Come on, boy. Help the gentleman choose his birds."

Henry, remembering the fiasco the first time he tried to grab an irate goose, did better this time. The farmer picked out fifty of the best looking ones and between them Henry and the two men drove the birds into a wooden pen.

Apparently satisfied, the farmer went indoors for his money.

Torse looked swiftly up and down the yard, caught sight of a lame looking goose flopped in the entrance, and pointed urgently: "Now, boy! Now!"

"What?" said Henry, startled.

"Pull out a good one – and shove in that lame one!"

Henry gaped. "But he'll know!"

"Stop blathering! Get hold before he's back!"

Henry did not fancy being confronted by an angry farmer. "Nay, you do it!"

Torse swore. Quickly his shillelagh appeared. "Get that bird now or I'll belt ya!" He brandished the club in Henry's face.

Furious, Henry lunged at the tired goose and thrust it into the pen. Torse for his part, snatched up the plumpest looking bird there and the switch was made.

"He'll kill us when he sees!"

"He'll never notice."

"It's only got one eye."

"And how does that matter!"

Their flurried expressions did not go unnoticed. "These is mine, is they?" said the farmer on his return. He looked sharply at the birds as he counted them. He paused when he came to twenty-one.

"Nay, I isn't having this un, you thieving Irish devil!"

"Oh, your honour 'tis a mistake, a mistake!" cried Torse quickly. He dived in and seized the skinny bird. "You imbecile!" he snapped at Henry. "What did you put this one in for?"

"Me? I never . . ."

Torse thrust the bird at Henry. "Don't let me catch you cheating good customers again!"

The drover turned to the farmer. "I'll choose you a good one meself, I will! There's no trusting young lads these days."

The farmer's scowl grew blacker. "If these birds isn't good uns I'll screw off your lugs! You and the lad."

"Of course, your honour, of course. You'd surely be right to."

Torse stared at Henry as if to turn him to stone.

Henry clutched the one-eyed goose and hurried out onto the track. The drover's warning in the Doss came back to him. Torse was not to be trusted. Henry knew that now for sure.

8

Black Jock

Trouble did not come all at once. The geese padded along for much of the afternoon as Henry drove them towards Abbeytown. The place turned out to be a village despite its name.

"Hah!" grunted Torse morosely. "Four o'clock and everyone asleep!"

But it was not true. Down a huddled line of houses a door opened and a face appeared; then another door opened and the drover began to cheer up. Soon he was transformed, warmly praising the merits of his geese to the villagers. Henry trailed with the flock as Torse sold eleven birds.

Henry was standing at a corner in the road with Moss alongside when a smartly dressed man came up to him. "And how much are your geese, my lad?"

Henry looked for Torse but the drover was at a door talking. He eyed the man's clothes. How much was Torse charging? Henry took a chance.

"Two and sixpence," he blurted out.

"Ah, yes. And are they good birds?"

"Irish," said Henry. "You'll not find better fatteners.

Ready by Christmas."

"Is that so? Then I'll take that big one."

It was a good-looking bird. They got it out of the flock between them.

"I've got a string," Henry told him. He fished a small lasso from his pocket, already made for just such a moment, slipping it over the bird's neck.

"Now you can walk it," he explained.

"So I can!" The man smiled and left Henry holding a bright half-crown piece.

Henry was glowing. Two shillings and sixpence! He knew he had done well. With the coin buried deep in his pocket, he waved at Moss to move in behind the flock and they got it moving again.

Torse was soon there. "Sold one, did you?"

"He paid me a half-crown," said Henry proudly.

The drover stared as if seeing him for the first time. "Then where is it?"

Henry showed him the shiny coin.

"That's twelve birds sold. Hah!" Torse snatched it off him. He was almost cackling. "Now let's get on. Carlisle's a long way yet."

Henry was indignant.

"What about my share?" he demanded. "I got us an extra tanner."

Torse glared. "Your share? Holy Mother! Whose birds are they?"

"But I got sixpence more than you."

"Did you now! Well get on down the road, or you'll not see a penny when we're done!"

We'll see about that, thought Henry. Part of that sixpence should have been his!

The flock reached a short track leading up to a farm.

"Just what we want!" Torse exclaimed. "Tonight we'll sleep in comfort."

Henry stared at the buildings and was less sure. Everything about the farm seemed to be uncared for. Sagging roofs, broken fencing, a cobbled yard thick in mud. But Torse blandly ignored it all. Assuming his most genial expression he banged on the house door.

An enormous bellied man looked out. Despite the drovers' unkempt appearance the man did not seem surprised.

"Oh yes, with the geese are you?"

He listened agreeably, and then led them across to a stone barn. "You can sleep in here, if it'll suit, and the geese can rest alongside in the paddock. Got a dog as well, eh?"

"A most valuable worker!" gushed Torse in his warmest manner.

The night's stay would cost a goose. Henry, relieved to find he would not be sleeping in a ditch, drove the birds into the paddock and all seemed well.

But it wasn't. They made an unwelcome discovery; the drovers had not got the barn to themselves. A smell of cooking wafted out of a corner where a dark figure crouched in the gloom. It was a tramp. The man was holding a tin lid over a candle and was frying an egg. His eyes glittered as he saw them.

"So, who's this, then?" the tramp demanded. "*Company* is it! Joining Black Jock? And *Irish* company at that – Torse the Goose is it not! And a little runt for company with him! Well now, we'll have to behave us if it's the Irish, won't we! Us can't be upsetting the Irish!"

Henry bridled. Torse glowered. Dismally the drover

recognised the tramp of old, and the man was well named. A mane of thick black hair down the back of his neck and heavy stubble gave him a dark brooding appearance.

Henry found himself steered clear by Torse and pushed down onto the hay against the far wall.

"What's the matter? Who is he?"

"A troublemaker," hissed Torse worriedly. "He needs watching. Keep the dog on a string. We want no trouble."

"I isn't scared of him!"

"Don't you shift from this side!"

Henry tied a string round Moss's neck and made him lie down in the hay.

Black Jock did not seem to stop staring. After a while Torse rose to go outside. "Don't be moving a single inch," he warned Henry. He was swinging his shillelagh.

Somewhere distantly a cow bellowed, otherwise there was silence. The tramp seized the moment. He threw his tin crashing into a corner.

"What're you staring at, you little toad?"

Henry huddled deeper down, gripping Moss. "I isn't staring, mister, I'm just looking."

The man loomed over him. "So, a Cumberland runt is you!" He seized Henry by his hair. "Tell me! What's your mate got hidden in his coat?"

"Ow, stop! You're hurting!"

Moss began to growl.

"A pouch, got a fat pouch, has he?"

Black Jock's face came closer, so close Henry could see a wart through the hair on the man's upper lip.

"You've seen his money pouch, haven't you? Where's he keep it?"

"I don't know, mister. I've seen no money or owt."

"You're lying, you little maggot! As sure as I'm Black Jock e's money on 'im"

Desperately Henry stared at the empty doorway. Where was Torse? Yes, he had seen a money pouch when the drover had paid the farmer in the field.

A cough sounded outside. Swiftly the man let go.

Torse sank down. "Not bothering you, is he?" He spoke in a low voice.

Deep within him Henry was trembling. For an instant he almost told about the pouch but he thought better of it. "He don't stop staring."

"Never you mind him, boy," said Torse confidingly. "I've been a-counting the geese to be sure."

They settled in the dark and Henry dug deeper into the hay. For a long time he lay awake, uneasily aware of the figure slumped by the opposite wall. Were they in danger? The reappearance of Torse's shillelagh seemed ominous.

Henry searched through his pockets and found a last piece of biscuit.

"Are you feeding that damn dog?" hissed Torse as he heard the crunching.

"It's hungry!"

"I'll kick it out tomorrow. Wasting good food!"

Henry bridled. He did not know whether he disliked Torse more than Black Jock. Both were hateful.

He sank into a troubled sleep, a hand locked on the dog's scruff.

For several hours no one stirred and not until the night was at its blackest did the tramp rise and creep out of the door. He was not missed until dawn when the drover went out for a pee.

Torse counted them again. "Curse him! I'll kill the

thieving rat!"

Henry stared round the farmyard. There was no sign of Black Jock, nor of the goose he had stolen. They counted the birds twice and each time were one short. Henry was glad it wasn't the limper. As it was, remembering Torse's words, he kept Moss on a string. Black Jock had been bad enough, but he didn't exactly trust the drover either.

9

Beggars' Breakfast

The geese were behaving badly, waddling off in wrong directions and Henry and Moss were finding it hard to keep them moving forward. Nor was Torse helping. The drover kept halting in the road and peering at the nearest hedge, then he would scratch around in the verge before setting off again. It seemed to happen every time they were near a cottage.

"What's the matter? What are you looking for?" Henry demanded.

The drover's unshaven face swung towards him. "Signs, boy. Signs!"

Signs? Henry could see no signs. Annoyed, he urged the geese on. Yet he did not stay annoyed for long. It was a brilliant day, the sky a vast open world with not a cloud in sight. Slowly they drove the flock through the hamlet of Moss Side and soon afterwards, as they reached a faded house, Torse halted yet again. This time though it was different. His manner had changed.

"Now, then, we have it!" he exclaimed excitedly. His eyes lit up. "We're in luck."

He was examining the ground by the garden gate.

"It's a good one."

Henry saw nothing to make him excited, then Torse pointed to three tiny twigs. They lay side-by-side down in among the leaves and were so small that Henry had easily missed them, though he saw them clearly now. They were neatly tied together with a strand of dried grass.

The drover cackled with delight. "I teld you, didn't I?"

Puzzled Henry touched the twigs with his fingertips. "What are they for?"

"Listen, boy. Are you stupid? Do you want to eat or don't you?"

Torse's voice dropped. He spoke quickly. It was the gypsies' code, their secret code. It told others on the road which were the good houses, and which to avoid. A scratch on a stone. A broken twig. Or grass twisted in a certain plait, or crossed. All were signs. Some warned travellers of danger; or to keep away, but three twigs tied side by side meant a chance of food or drink. This cottage was a good one.

"Now get to the door and knock," Torse ordered. "And don't be looking cheerful or they'll give you nothing!"

Henry experienced a moment of panic. "Ain't you coming with me?"

"That I am not! I'll take the dog and stay with the geese. But wait till I's gone! A nice innocent child is what's needed . . . a sweet innocent face."

The cottage door was ajar.

"Tell 'em we 'asn't eaten anything these past two days."

Henry was shocked. "But we have! We ate at that woman's."

"And how will they know a thing like that?"

Torse started the flock moving, chuckling inwardly. A

young hungered face would melt the coldest heart.

Scowling, Henry waited till the drover had moved on along the road. Somehow he didn't want the man watching him. Full of doubt, he went up the path.

"Droving, are you! My, and you so young!" said the woman. She was in her thirties and held a cat under one arm. A brush covered in cat hairs was in her other hand. Henry's first thought was that she looked like a teacher, except that she would have been at school if she had been.

"It's just a cup of tea, missis," he said, embarrassed.

She laughed at his shy manner. "Then it's lucky I have the kettle on, isn't it! Come on inside."

Before Henry realised how it had happened he found himself sitting at a white-scrubbed kitchen table eating a huge breakfast. Between mouthfuls of bacon and egg he told her all about the journey. How he didn't know what was going to happen once he got to Carlisle. How Torse, who was a real drover, was sometimes all right and sometimes lost his temper, but usually was all right when his tooth was not hurting, which it did a lot.

"Carlisle! My, that's miles away!" She sounded admiring. "And what do they call you then? *Henry!* Well fancy that, would you believe it, one of my cats is called Henry!"

She grinned at him and he grinned back. Somehow he felt he had made a friend. He liked her a lot.

"I've got a dog and he's called Moss," he confessed. "He's like a sheepdog."

"Is he? Then you are lucky for sheepdogs are very intelligent."

Not until he had eaten every scrap off the plate and wiped it with a piece of bread did Henry suffer a pang of guilt as he remembered Torse.

She listened solemnly.

"I mean, I didn't mean to eat it all . . ."

"That's quite all right," she told him. "It's quite understandable. If you wait a minute."

She went back into the kitchen.

To his surprise as he left she shook his hand. Never before had anyone shaken Henry by his hand.

He remembered the time Torse had knocked at a door. *"Tis a goodly house you keep,"* he recited in what he hoped was the right voice, *"and I thanks ya for it."*

"Why, how kind of you," she said, laughing, then seeing him hesitate: "Is there anything else . . ."

"I just wondered, are you a teacher?"

"Why yes, that *is* clever of you. But I'm at home because I've been poorly."

"I thought you was," said Henry, pleased with himself. "A teacher, I mean."

As he hurried off to catch up with the flock she called: "You must visit me again."

Not until he had gone nearly a quarter of a mile did he realise that she was almost the first person who had not remarked about his bare feet. That showed how good she was.

The warmth of the packet stole through his trouser pocket. A butty for the road, she had said. Well he'd save half for Torse and the other half for Moss. That would be fair.

Thinking this, he stopped to break it in two but really he knew already what would happen. Torse would grab both pieces and eat them himself . . . Henry grinned. This time it would be different. He walked more slowly and now it was his turn to search carefully in the hedgerows.

The geese were round a bend gorging on the verges.

"Oh! So you're back, are you! And you got a free breakfast!"

Torse was slumped by a signpost looking angry.

"You got inside the door quick enough!"

Henry protested: "She said I'd to go in."

"Bacon and eggs, eh! And tea . . . a *pot* full! Plenty of everything, I suppose! And me starving and wondering if you've gone and been a-murdered."

"She would never murder anyone!" said Henry, upset at the thought. "Anyway, you said the gypsy sign at the gate was a good one, so it's not my fault!"

The drover had no answer to that.

"Juicy bacon, was it?"

Thick eyebrows swivelled towards him.

Henry was enjoying this. He laid it on. "Proper juicy! And fried bread. And buttered toast. *And* three sugars in my tea!"

"Hah!"

"Anyway, I told her how we was walking the geese and everything and she could hardly believe all the geese we have."

"She's a silly stupid woman," snapped Torse.

Henry glared. "She's not! She's a teacher. You've not even met her!"

"Don't have no time for teachers! Too clever by half. Next time try using your brain and get a bite for me or you'll be getting no pay!"

That did it. Angrily Henry rummaged inside his jacket. "I've just remembered. I've got summat!"

He produced the butty.

"There's half for you and . . ."

Torse snatched both halves. Henry had known he would.

."A bacon butty! Hah! Hiding it was you!"

He wolfed it down, at the same time congratulating himself on his shrewdness. There was nothing like a sweet innocent face.

But the drover was not alone in shrewdness. Henry grinned to himself. Torse had not even bothered to say thank you. Not that that mattered, it was enough just to watch the drover eating his slug and bacon butty.

10

A Biff on the Chin

Henry longed for the evening to arrive so they could stop and light a fire. A chill wind was blowing and it cut through his clothes. Even Torse in his heavy coat was looking pinched. But in other ways it was a good day. Three stops at small farms resulted in sixty-five birds being sold; and Moss was proving how good he was at droving the geese. Henry was surprised at the way he seemed to guess the flock's erratic movements and kept the birds moving forward.

A friendly smiling woman let them into a paddock where they now squatted. "We calls it Goose Field," she told them, and generously let them off with a mere two pence for the night. Torse flopped to the ground sighing with relief. And that was all that seemed to happen.

Henry, hoping that something would, did not improve matters by asking the wrong thing.

"When are we going to eat . . . I mean eat *proper?*"

Torse flinched. He was staring hard at various plump birds.

"Well, I'm *hungry.*"

"Boy, you ate this morning!"

"But that was hours ago."

"Was it! Well all we've got left is a brew, so you can shut up! Now go a find wood for a fire!"

That at least was something to do. He raided the hedges and soon they had a good blaze going. As they grew warmer, Henry sought out the one-eyed goose. He lifted it clear of the others and after a feeble tussle got it into a comfortable hold under one arm. He could see now why it was limping for its left leg was twisted. Gripping the bird firmly he pressed several small twigs against the limb and bound them round with a piece of string so that it made a tight splint. Then he tied a loop of string round the bird's neck so he could pick it out easily.

"And what's that nonsense?"

The drover switched his glare.

"I'm mending its leg. Five twigs for luck."

"Oh *are* you! Well you can stop that. What's more, as we is peckish and you is looking nasty, pretending I never feed you, I'm thinking we'll rummage this lame one and have done with it."

His eyes fixed on the bird.

Henry was shocked. "You won't," he said defiantly. "And it's not lame."

"Oh?" Torse's eyebrows shot up. "And who says I won't?"

"I do . . ." began Henry.

At once the drover lunged.

This time Henry was quicker. Grasping the goose, he lowered his head and more by good luck than anything he biffed the drover on the chin. Torse was shocked. Despite the size of his coat, the man was unusually light and with a yell he pitched over sideways.

"Oooof! Beat me would you!"

Henry did not flinch. "Don't come near, or I'll do it again!"

This was something new. The drover got to his feet warily. Despite his thinness the boy was stronger than he looked.

"Jaysus, you've ruined my coat!"

He had landed in a green splat of goose dirt.

"I mean it," cried Henry again. He tried not to sound shrill. His heart was pounding as he held on to the goose. Whatever happened he was not going to let go of the bird. "Keep back!"

Torse hesitated for once unsure what to do. He thought to reach for his shillelagh, yet something made him pause. He knew he could easily knock the boy flat in the dust but that would be no good because then he would have to walk the flock by himself.

His voice turned deceptively quiet. "All right, boy, all right . . . no need to fight, now, have we?"

A flicker of a smile lit his face. "Won't do us any good, now will it! We men of the road we must stick together mustn't we!"

Henry was angry and not sure that they must.

But Torse went on, his eyes glinting. "You go and get us some water and I'll make us a good tin of tea. We'll have us a good sweet brew."

"I'm not leaving the goose!" said Henry defiantly. He knew what would happen if he did. "And I don't want no tea. I'm always fetching stupid water!"

"Don't want no tea? Of course you do!" Momentarily Torse seemed about to lose his temper again, but he went on: "I told you before we set out didn't I? *You* cart the water and I make the tea. And don't you be fretting for the pretty goose. Torse don't want it, he don't. You leave it safe here with me. What we want is a good brew."

Henry kept the bird under one arm and grabbed the tin. Wanted tea, did he! Wanted to kill the goose. Given the chance he knew Torse would do just that. Well he would show him!

"Moss, come on!"

"Just you leave the bird," snapped Torse. "It'll be nice and safe."

But Henry didn't leave it. The dog at his heels, he searched for nearly half a mile before he found a spring at the roadside. He released the goose. A sandstone step had been let into the ground to make the spring easier to reach. The water was bubbling but it was a brackish brown. Just perfect. He had a long drink then he filled the tin almost to the top. Torse wanted a good brew did he, well he'd get one all right! Suddenly determined, he held the tin steady and peed into it until it was full.

11

Hurried Exit

Henry was the first to realise something strange was happening. The geese were plodding along surprisingly well, almost too well, almost quickly. Even the limper seemed to be moving faster than usual. Somehow it was not normal. Henry tried to tell Torse but the drover had sighted a huddle of roofs ahead and was gloating at the thought of nearing an inn. The man was also trying to recall a half-forgotten reason why there was need for caution.

"Newton Arlosh! What is it about Newton Arlosh?"

Henry hadn't the faintest idea.

"The geese . . . "

"Not now, boy, not now."

But Henry persisted. "Summat funny's going on. Why don't ya listen!"

The drover slapped his coat. "That's it! It's the pond! We've gotta keep the geese off the pond!"

Henry stared open mouthed.

"We gotta keep 'em out of the water!"

The man was barmy! "Geese *likes* water. Everyone knows geese likes water!"

Torse was disgusted at Henry's ignorance.

"Of course they do! But water doesn't like geese, does it? Water takes the nice juicy fat off 'um! Don't sell well then, do they . . . too thin looking.

"Look sharp! They're off!"

As if at a signal the geese started to move more purposefully. Their necks were craning forward as if in a race.

Henry took one look and ran to head them off.

"They've got the scent!"

The geese had more than that. The birds had seen the pond. It was overlooked by a small fortified church with a stubby tower.

In an excited rush they padded forward. At the same time as the leaders headed for the water a rebel group went through an open gate into the churchyard.

"I'll get 'em!" shouted Henry.

But he was not the first there. A black and white dog raced ahead and was over the wall in a moment. Henry arrived to find geese in among the tombstones gulping down bowls of flowers. At the same time a breakaway group raced out of sight behind the church.

Seconds later, surprisingly, they reappeared. Moss was there, weaving to and fro driving them back.

Henry laughed delighted. "Did you see?" he cried as the birds regained the road. "Moss got 'em out again."

But Torse had given up on the geese and had flopped by the pond.

For a while man and boy watched the ecstatic splashing, and gradually Torse became more cheerful as his own thirst developed. He rose to his feet.

"Time for a quencher! Stay with 'em, boy. We'll stop the night."

He went off full of anticipation. His memory had usefully improved. The good old *Joiner's Arms* lay just round a bend in the road.

Henry lay back with Moss at his side and watched the birds. Droving was better than he had imagined. The one bad thing was he was hungry again, really hungry. Only the geese seemed to be well fed.

Torse's visit to the inn went wrong. Talk filled the place. As he moved towards the bar some instinct made him examine the customers more carefully. For the first time he noticed two men talking at a table in a corner, two figures as ragged as himself. He paused, dismayed.

He scurried back along the road.

"Get up!" he yelled. "Get up! We're going!"

Henry sat up, startled. "Going?"

"Yes, going! Are you deaf!"

"But you said we was stopping the night!"

Torse's face was covered in sweat.

"Well we're not," he blustered. "It's too early! Now get the flock moving *quickly!* Towns are terrible bad places for geese!"

Henry gaped. Towns? What towns? They were going to a town.

Already the drover was half way round the pond, chivvying the birds to get them started.

"Come on, boy! Don't just stand there!"

Henry hurried after him.

In a ragged movement the geese set off through the village. "Keep 'em going!" Torse urged.

"But why aren't we stopping?" called Henry.

The drover offered no explanation. He plodded on, and

Henry was shocked. He realised that Torse was frightened.

This thought might easily have spoiled the rest of the day except for the simplest of occurrences. The track divided into two and Henry, without thinking, drove the flock into the smaller less obvious way before he wondered if he had made a mistake.

But he hadn't. Everything changed. The stony road was turning into a sandy track. Overgrown hedges formed an inviting green tunnel.

Torse's anxious stare changed. A dawning look of realisation came over him as the geese padded along. "Bless us! I'd gone and forgotten, I had. This is the old Irish Road!"★

He stared at Henry.

"The secret road," he explained.

"I know," said Henry, though he didn't.

"You know? Oh, you *know,* do you?" Torse glared. "I suppose you know everything, you being so clever? And I'm here knowing nothing?"

Henry went red.

"I mean I've heard me brother talking," lied Henry.

Torse was indignant. "Heard lots, you have, but not about the Irish Road! Not the *secret road*. We Irish have walked this road with geese and cattle for hundreds of years, we have. That's one thing you didn't know, boy!"

"It can't be hundreds."

"Longer! Listen, boy, I'm learning you terrible secrets, I am."

Henry sniffed disbelievingly and stared at the track winding away before them. "I bet there's no one as calls it Irish, not anyone."

★ A different verson of the Irish Road still existed decades later.

"Wrong you are again! All the way to Carlisle. Everybody knows it! And you'll not find one signpost standing along the whole way with words on it to say so. It's a drover's secret."

Henry didn't believe a word. He knew it couldn't be all the way to Carlisle. He was getting used to ignoring the drover's odd ways. Even so, the secret road or track, whether Henry believed in it or not was easier underfoot. Away to the north now lay the glistening marshes and the Solway Firth with the blur of Scotland rising beyond; to the south lay the Lakeland mountains, deceptively bright, yet still seeming far off. Ahead lay Carlisle though it was still beyond the horizon.

Soon they began to meet other travellers. A pedlar appeared; and a man with a pig on a string; then a scissors grinder, pushing a one-wheeled cart. After that, two women in speckled apron dresses and clogs on their way home after weeding a field.

Irish road? More a Cumberland one, muttered Henry. But the truth was that both he and Torse were now in a better mood and trivial though it might be, the little track had brought it about.

The sea of geese, many of them flagging wearily, reached a remote spot called Longlands. At sight of an ivy-covered dwelling the drover's face lit up.

"Tyson's cottage. The very same."

Skilfully Henry steered the flock into a field. The cottager, a roadman till he had grown too old for brooming, recognised the drover from previous years. Torse sacrificed a goose in exchange for the night's stay and some generous hunks of bread and cheese.

"We'll have us a brew. But go and find better water this time," he warned Henry.

They supped their tea and Henry flopped down into a ditch. Soon he was joined by the ever-silent Moss.

"You don't bark much, do ya?" He picked briars out of the dog's coat. "You're a good 'un!"

For the first time Moss had begun to wag his tail. Not much, but it was a good sign. Henry regarded him as much a part of the journey now as he was himself. A goose dog, that was it, a sheepdog and a goose dog.

As it grew dark Torse retreated into his den. "It'll be good going now all the way to Carlisle, boy!" he predicted smugly.

12

Door Knocking

But everything did not continue to go well. Nor did the drover's good mood last.

"Well it's not my fault!" yelled Henry.

"It is, boy, it is! You eat too much!"

"I does not!"

"You got worms, you have! We had good bread and cheese. What more do you want?"

"That was last night!" yelled Henry. He stamped furiously. "I'm hungry *now.*"

It was already ten in the morning. They had walked the geese since eight without a proper halt. Henry was beginning to feel hollow.

Both were still smarting as they reached little Kirkbride village. Torse waved a hand.

"If you're that hungry go and knock along them doors. And don't start looking cheerful, or they'll give you nothing!"

Henry glared. He looked anything but cheerful.

At the first cottage a small unsmiling girl confronted him. She stood in the doorway, her legs screwed up, her cotton dress all a-twist.

"And we hasn't eaten proper for two whole days," Henry was explaining, but the child did not answer. "A sweet brew of tea, miss, is all we is wanting, if ya could be so . . ."

The girl began to wet her knickers.

Henry retreated, shame-faced.

Torse had failed to find anything on his side. "We isn't doing well," he snapped.

"I'm real hungry."

"And you think I'm not!"

"Starving," said Henry. "And so is Moss."

"Your stupid dog's nothing to do with me!"

"He's not stupid!"

As he spoke the geese went wild. In a rush a deluge of fighting bodies began to devour a flowerbed outside a cottage.

"Stop them! Stop them!" yelled Torse.

Henry took one look and didn't even try.

The feast lasted until a door burst open. An enraged man tore out brandishing a broom. His face was crimson.

"Get off with you!" he yelled, swiping at the birds. "It'll be me gun next time!"

"Go boil your head!" bawled Torse.

Somehow they got the flock to the far end of the village without a crust begged or a goose sold.

Torse was still muttering dark thoughts about Kirkbride as they reached an isolated cottage. Henry didn't wait for the drover to tell him what to do, he knocked over-hard at the door feeling bad tempered. Already it was afternoon.

A chubby faced man looked out.

"Hello? And who are you?" The man was unbuttoning his postman's coat. "Oh yes, selling geese are you? Well you are lucky catching me in. Just doing a brew I am!"

Swiftly Henry found himself thrust aside. Torse's dour

expression had evaporated.

"Bless you, sir, you've read our very minds! Me poor frail young friend here is fairly fainting for want of a drink, he is, and a touch of 'uman kindness."

"Nay, is that so?"

The frail young thing glowered, but to his surprise Torse's unashamed begging worked. The postman took in their ragged appearance and disappeared into his kitchen saying "Back in a minute!" and soon the drovers were perched on a wall eating cheese butties and balancing mugs of tea.

"This'll keep you going a bit," said the postman warmly.

"Bless you, sir. You're a true fellow man!"

The postman eyed Moss.

"And who else is hungry?" He disappeared again and reappeared holding a bowl of meal. "Here, ya are boy."

Moss wolfed it down as if he had not eaten for weeks.

"My own Bessy died just a month ago," the postman explained. "You miss your dog. They get to be one of the family."

This generous encounter encouraged an unexpected if temporary change in Torse's mood. As they bade the postman goodbye and set off again Torse was almost affable.

"Funny thing it is, walking the geese," he confessed. "Some days there's nothing happens and the birds go nicely. But other days, there's nothing but trouble, and me wondering why I ever left Ireland."

He clutched at his bandaged jaw.

"Course, it isn't all good at home. Me old mother working every hour there is, scrubbing the floors, and me earning the pennies, digging the drains. All work it is."

Henry listened. He knew it was the same for lots of them. "*My* mum takes in washing," he confessed.

"Does she now! A washerwoman? Well that's good clean work."

But Henry knew it wasn't always good. "She gets ill sometimes. When she does too much. She got ill all last winter."

"Did she now?" The drover rubbed his hairy chin. "Then there's a thing for a young fella like you to be thinking about – getting your mother away from all that work in her old age."

Henry had thought about it already in a hopeless sort of way. But what chance was there? He knew she felt lucky to have work. Some folk hadn't any. One thing he was sure about, nothing good would happen with Nathan around.

As if he had read Henry's thoughts the drover said: "And what's it with your step-da?"

Henry frowned. He did not like talking about Nathan.

"He's a big man," said Torse.

Henry said: "He hits us. Me anyway. He'd be better if he had a job."

That was what mother was always saying.

Torse turned to look at a field. "Here's a good spot."

He peered through a gap in the hedge, and quickly pulled back. "Oh, God save us! It isn't!"

Henry pushed forward to look for himself.

"Tis the Ghost Field!"

Trees sheltered two sides of a small paddock. It had an air of being closed in, protective, with a glint of water at the far end, ideal for the night. Yet Torse hesitated, then with an "Oh, nothing will happen!" he waved at Henry to steer the birds in.

But his manner remained cautious.

"Ghost field?" said Henry.

"Tis nothing, boy, nothing . . . take no notice."

Then seeing Henry was still listening: "Well, if you must know, old Jason Lobby, out of Belfast he was. He come here like always with the geese, walking the long miles by night to this very field. And one night this side of Greenspot he sees a light is following him. Strange it was, kept on and on, just following, scaring him terrible, like it's got a great white face with no body. But a mouth, oh a long mouth that opens and closes like it's going to speak . . .

"Then he meets two fellas and they see he's frighted. 'We'll go with you, Jason', they say, but hardly ten steps taken and a fearsome light is shining and Jason he drops dead just like that! Them two fellas was scared I can tell you! Next morning Jason's body is here in the ditch, a great green frog stuffed down his throat, and the geese all gone everywhere."

Henry stared at the hedgerow. The hair on his neck had turned prickly. "What was the light?"

"Terrible it was. Like a bog spirit, rising out of the black earth."

Henry listened, not wanting to believe the drover but feeling nervous all the same. He began to gather up stones. Avoiding the ditch where the body had been found, he moved to the safety of another one further away. He searched along it for frogs, then sank down in the grasses and with Moss at his side kept a nervous watch.

No ghost appeared but a restless night followed. Earlier than usual the drovers got away, setting off through the dawn haze.

"I don't believe in ghosts," Henry told the drover.

"No," said Torse. "Nor me, unless I sees one."

"I had some stones ready," Henry said. And then, seeing the drover did not understand: "For throwing."

"You done right, boy. You done right."

13

A Bossy Girl

Henry was sent to a farm to fill the water tin.

"Make sure you taste it afore you bring it!" warned Torse. "And while you are there be asking if they want some geese! Good Irish fatteners. Tell 'em how they're cheap and how good they is."

"I *know*, I *know*," said Henry. Why did the man keep on?

The farm had a prosperous look, painted shutters and a small walled garden with blue gates. Henry went up a track at the side and knocked at the back door. A girl about his own age opened it. She had a black mourning band fastened round a sleeve of her dress showing someone had died.

He waved his empty tin.

"Can I have some water?"

She stared and did not answer so that Henry, feeling he had been abrupt, added: "I'm with the geese."

"Jenny, who is it?"

A woman came through the kitchen. She had a sad face and looked as if she had been weeping.

Henry said: "It's just water I'm needing missis, and would you be wanting to buy any geese to fatten for Christmas? I'm walking 'em to Carlisle market."

The woman paused distractedly then shook her head. "I've no time for geese today, but you can have water."

Henry stared through the kitchen to a room across the passage and caught his breath. A coffin was on the table with the lid off. The last coffin he had seen had been his father's and then only at a distance. This one was small and he wondered if there were a body in it.

"Jenny, take him to the pump."

The girl led across the yard. Her hair hung down her back in a long single tress and was tied with a scarlet ribbon.

"Haven't you got no clogs?" she asked. Hers were clean and shiny.

"I don't need any," said Henry.

She eyed his tangled hair. "Your hair needs cutting."

"It don't! My hair's all right."

She sniffed her disapproval.

"Anyway, how far have you walked?"

"All the way from Silloth. And I'm going all the way to Carlisle."

He was proud of that.

"I heard the geese."

"Aye. I've a lot. Hundreds."

Her passive face broke into disbelief. "You can't manage hundreds. Not by yourself."

"I does so!"

"You tell lies. There's a man. I've seen him!"

Henry flushed. "Well we've sold some. I'm getting good at selling 'em."

She straightened her head so that she stood a shade taller. "You brag, too."

"What if I do, it's nowt to do with you."

"You're wanting our water, so that's to do with us. I hope your tin is clean."

Henry scowled. She sounded bossy. He didn't like bossy girls.

They stopped against a wall at a cast iron pump. A deep stone trough stood below the spout.

"How old are you?" she asked.

"Thirteen."

"Why aren't you at school?"

"I got special permission, so I can be a drover."

"I'm going to the hirings to get a job," she told him, "when I'm old enough."

"I know all about hirings and getting a job."

"There you are again. You're a bragger. Hold your tin under the spout properly."

She took hold of the long handle and began to pump it up and down. Gurgling sounded from down in the pipe and then in a rush a cascade of water poured out over Henry.

"Ow!" he yelled, jumping back. "You did that on purpose."

"I never did," laughed the girl. "Anyway you stink!"

"I'm wet through!"

"No you're not! It's just a splash."

"Do ya want thumping!"

"Try it and you'll get one back! Anyway, come on, we'd best go round the side of the house 'cause of visitors."

"Whose is the coffin?" said Henry.

The girl stared with a blank expression. "It's my aunt's new baby. It's died of a weak chest."

Henry looked scornful. "Babies don't get weak chests."

"Yes they do. Little Annie had one."

"Well they don't die of 'em. My brother's got a weak

chest and he hasn't died."

"Annie did. She got whooping cough and was only four months old. Anyway, your brother was lucky."

Henry stared round the cobbled yard. The house stood with two good stone barns alongside it. The place looked well run. "It must be good living here."

"I don't live here. I'm only visiting because of little Annie dying. But I wouldn't mind living here."

They reached the gate into the lane. "Are you going to come back this way?"

"I don't know. I might."

She gave him a faint smile.

Henry set off with the water as Moss came bounding up to meet him.

"Oh, whose is the dog?"

"He's mine! He's called Moss."

She called from the gate.

"What's yours?"

Henry did not reply. He concentrated on keeping the tin level and carried it all the way to the camp without spilling any. The coffin had been tiny.

Torse was feeding a fire with twigs.

"What you been doing? Having a bath?"

"It was the pump. I got splashed."

"Do they want any geese?"

Henry shook his head.

"No? Did you ask 'em proper?"

"Course I did."

He was going to tell him about the baby and the coffin but Torse was not listening. They were in a good spot on a patch of rough land and had boxed the geese in between two walls.

The drover examined the tin. "You tasted it like I teld you?"

"Of course," lied Henry.

"Then we'll have us a brew. It's been a long day."

A long day, and drizzle in the night. Henry woke soaked and cold. He curled up tighter and kept Moss alongside to help stay warm. In the ragged light of a new day they set off with the flock under a grey sky, the geese in a contrary mood. Hardly thirty yards along the road the leading birds reached a minor junction and began to turn down a rutted lane.

"Stop 'em!" yelled Torse. "That's the wrong way!"

Henry set off at a run.

Cackling erupted as the geese encountered a new threat. Two pony-drawn carts appeared behind the column. To the drovers' dismay they began to force a way through.

"Stop! Stop!" yelled Torse.

Henry realised it was a funeral procession. The carts and their ponies halted in the middle of a sea of geese.

"Get on theer!" shouted the leading driver. He cracked his whip over the birds, glowering angrily at Torse.

Torse took one look and crossed himself several times.

White faces stared down from under giant umbrellas. Sandwiched high up on a seat behind the driver of the first cart were a man and a woman with a girl squashed between them. Henry caught her glance but her face remained impassive. Lying in the well of the cart was the tiny coffin covered with canvas. A second cart followed, full of people. All were wearing black.

Muddled moments ensued before the cortege got through and only as it began to emerge into the clear road did Henry suddenly push forward.

"It's Henry," he called.

The girl did not look back.

"It's *Henry!*"

The carts rolled away.

A hard time beset the drovers as the wayward geese were rounded up. It was a miserable morning with the rain growing heavier.

"Don't care, do they!" grumbled Torse. "Drive right through us! Never a thought about us poor drovers. *Rubbish* we are!"

"It was a funeral," said Henry. "There was a coffin."

"I don't care if it was *two* funerals."

Henry, his hair sodden and streaky, was shocked. He wafted a drip off the end of his nose.

"It was a dead baby," he explained.

They trailed back and forth after the strays. The day had started badly.

Later in the morning the rain stopped but not until mid-afternoon did they manage to beg two mugs of hot tea and start to feel warmer.

Torse paused in front of Henry looking very serious. "Been thinking I have, boy. Thinking how you want to be keeping away from the girls, you do."

Henry frowned. "I don't bother with 'em."

"Nothing but trouble, they are!"

The drover's remarks came after he had watched Henry stop to splash ditch water onto his face.

"What you doing that fool thing for?"

"Cause I stinks."

"Jaysus, didn't you get wet enough in the rain! Don't you know washing's dangerous?"

Henry ignored him. The girl had been right, he *did* stink.

He had told Torse so, hence the criticism.

"Can't we stop?"

"No we can't! We'll go another mile yet! So don't be thinking any more of those stupid thoughts."

But he had got it wrong. Half a mile further on one or two of the weaker birds began to flop. Each time it happened Henry or Torse picked up the weary bundle and carried it until another needed help.

Then the one-eyed goose went down. Henry got to it first, aware that Torse was eyeing the bird yet again.

"I'll have that in the pot yet," threatened the drover.

"You won't! It's done no harm!"

"What you doing now?"

Henry had grabbed up a fistful of grass.

"I'm feeding it."

"Feeding it! What you doing that dumb thing for! Geese feed themselves!"

"It's too thin," said Henry.

"Thin! Hah. That makes two of you. You're as stupid as the goose!"

Henry was angry. Why didn't the man leave the bird alone? He carried it till his arms ached. He would have to watch carefully; he knew that Torse could easily wring the bird's neck just like that.

"Now come on," ordered Torse. "Five days left. We don't wanna go missing the market. Go on, get a move on . . ."

For the second time in the hour he broke off mid-sentence and looked back. His manner was suddenly sharp and watchful.

Henry recognised the sign. "What is it?"

The drover squinted, his head aslant, listening. "It's

nothing! And keep your questions to yourself!"

"I was only asking!"

Torse set off anew but it was obvious to Henry that another moody change had come over the man. He was muttering again as he trailed the flock. Noticeably he avoided Henry's anxious glances.

The road was empty and lonely and at dusk they reached a patch of common ground and halted for the night. Henry was still no wiser about what was upsetting the man.

The attack took them by surprise.

14

Attacked

Terrified yells echoed through the gloom of the wood. Henry, his arms loaded with branches for the fire, turned cold with fright. It was Torse. But what was happening? He could hear several voices. Thinking fast, he set down the wood and began to crawl forward on hands and knees.

Three figures were standing by the fire.

"Remember me, do ya?" snarled the biggest man.

"Jergo . . . *Aaaah!*"

The blow landed in the drover's ribs.

"Aye, Jergo as is! Come to collect a little debt I has, with a pal along to see fair play!"

Henry moved nearer until he could see more clearly. He failed to recognise the man called Jergo but he knew the second one well enough. It was Black Jock.

"My money you windbag! Give me my money!"

"Jergo, *no* – I owe you nothin!"

"Liar! Four whole shillings and two pence. A night's cards lost! And you sliding away like the slimy toad you is!"

A fresh thud sounded followed by a yell of pain.

"For the love of God, don't!"

"Where's your money pouch, you rat!"

"Nowhere, I don't have no pouch . . . "

Another yell of pain ended the sentence.

"His coat," cried Black Jock. "The money will be in his coat."

"Then find it!"

Henry's heart was pounding. What could he do? There were two of them. If he could find the drover's shillelagh. It had been lying somewhere near the hedge.

Another thud! Torse's voice rose sharply.

Henry lay flat as a figure stumbled through the gloom. Black Jock came past, searching the ground.

The increasing darkness gave good cover. Henry closed his mind to the danger and tried to crawl nearer. If he could find the shillelagh at least he would be armed, and he was still thinking this as a better idea came. A much better one.

Upset by the noise, a rush of frightened geese hissed past. Quickly, Henry got in among them. He moved along now at a crouch and almost by the hedge he crawled over a ragged hump. Torse's coat! Excitedly he began to search for an inner pocket. As the geese hissed away, he moved on and rolled down into a ditch.

The men heard him.

"Someone's there!"

Jergo peered into the dark.

"'Tis the geese," said Black Jock.

"Where's the boy? You said there was a boy!"

"It ain't the boy, 'tis the geese!" Black Jock's voice rose excitedly. "Wait, it's here! I've found it! The old devil's coat!"

The men hurried to the fireside and tore at the garment,

cursing its layers. A stream of rags and papers fell out.

"Where's your pouch?" snarled Jergo. He shook the drover fiercely. "Where is it, you old devil? Tell us or I'll kill you!"

They were arguing angrily as a rock sang out of the night and struck Black Jock in the face. His shriek of pain was followed by another yell as a second stone hit Jergo.

"It's the boy! Get him!"

But it was easier said than done. The flock had scattered and each movement in the dark proved a false one for the robbers.

Another rock hurtled past and crashed in the scrub.

"Over there!"

In the blackness Henry kept in among the geese. His hand closed on another stone. A figure moved past the glowing remains of the campfire. Guessing at the man's movements he took aim. Another angry yell! Henry's years of practice throwing pebbles on the shore at Silloth were paying off.

Jergo snapped at Black Jock: "Shut your noise! *Listen!*"

Hooves sounded heavily on the road. Two candle lanterns wavered into sight and the dark form of a cart began to draw near. Timing it perfectly, Henry landed a rock in the heart of the fire sending a cascade of brilliant orange sparks up into the night. Cursing, the robbers let go of the drover as the glare lit the camp. At the same time a salvo of barking broke out. A black and white form raced out of the darkness. Henry turned, startled. It was Moss! The dog was tearing round the robbers barking furiously. The din proved too much for the men, dropping their sticks they turned and fled.

"Good boy!" cried a delighted Henry. "Good boy you've scared 'em!"

The cart did not stop. He listened to make sure the men had gone, and it seemed they had.

Several groans made him turn.

"Oh, Henry me lad, I's done for," wailed Torse.

The drover was in a pitiful way. His face and coat were spattered with blood. Gently Henry got a hand under one of the man's arms and helped him across to the remains of the fire.

"I's done for, I is!"

"No . . . no you're not!"

Henry never knew properly what to say if people spoke like this, but remembering how his mother dealt with most troubles, he searched quickly for the tin and Torse's bag of tea. Both lay where the robbers had hunted for the pouch.

He brought the drover's coat over and heaped it gently round the little man's shoulders. Then he went for wood and water and soon stoked the fire into a cheerful blaze.

Henry poured some water into a cloth.

"You'll 'ave to keep still."

He wiped at the blood on Torse's face.

"Thank you, boy, thank you. You're a godsend, you are – *Aaaah!* – And I owes you, I does, Torse the Goose owes you."

The drover seemed close to tears, for the moment at least. Despite all the blows, Torse's troublesome tooth had escaped untouched, but his pained expression showed it was hurting. Henry tore a new piece of rag out of the drover's coat and tied it round the man's jaw.

They supped the tea, and the drover began to search through his pockets.

"Not a penny left! The thieving divils have stolen every penny earned!"

Henry remembered the ditch. He crawled along the grassy tunnel looking.

"Is this it?"

The pouch was bulging with coins. Torse wept as he took hold. "God bless you, boy! Me pouch!"

He counted the money, and once he had done that he counted it a second time more slowly to make sure he had not miscounted.

"Are you a Catholic, boy? Ah, no, you're not. Well you can't be helping that; you'll have your reward in heaven just the same!"

It seemed fairly certain that Torse himself did not intend to be as generous as his maker. Even so Henry was pleased. Had the pouch gone missing then his own pay would have gone with it.

"Who was the other man?"

The drover's face screwed up. "The scum of the road. We don't want no more of him, or Black Jock either!"

A long restless night followed and daylight came amid groans of frustration. Despite the need to press on, Torse was too unwell to move. His chest and legs were badly bruised, his condition made worse by his aching tooth. Resigned, he sagged where he lay and gave up for the rest of the day.

"We must be watching, we must, and we must be listening," he warned Henry. "Them thieving rogues could land back, they could."

Henry did not like the sound of that. He set up a pile of stones in case the worst happened.

But the men did not reappear. Most of the time Torse slept, enveloped in his coat. Late in the afternoon Henry brewed a tin of tea and they ate the last of the cheese, sharing it with Moss.

"He really barked!" said Torse.

"Scared 'em, he did!"

"Never had a dog around afore," said Torse, still marvelling.

The long rest did the drover good. Next morning in better shape, he set off again, though slower than usual with more roadside halts, which suited both the geese and the drovers.

15

Boots of Good Fortune

Somewhere on the morning air came the chink of metal. Henry urged the geese on round a bend. The drovers had slept a stolen night in a field and at dawn had driven the birds back on to the track. Now they had reached a blacksmith's forge.

"'Ow do, then!"

The smith had been shoeing a heavy Clydesdale horse. He had a deep voice and was the strongest looking man Henry had ever seen, big and broad shouldered. The man eyed the sea of birds.

"Wanting boots for tha geese then!" he jested.

Henry grinned. "We gave 'em clogs back in Silloth. Tar ones!"

Torse not wanting to be left out wagged a grubby finger. "On our way to Carlisle market we are!"

The smith laughed and tethered the horse in the shade alongside the smithy. "Oh aye? Perhaps you've got a good 'un that would fit in our old oven?"

This kind of talk Torse enjoyed. In generous vein he picked out a bird for a bargain price of eighteen pence and the smith, recognising that it was thirsty work selling geese, brewed a companionable pot of tea for the three of them.

Henry sat in the door of the smithy clutching a steaming mug. He was impressed with the workshop. It might be good to become a blacksmith.

Big Jim, for so he was called, noticed his eager stare.

"Appen you'd be good at working the bellows, me lad?"

Would he! Henry was there in a moment. Following the smith's advice not to rush things, he started to pump steadily and soon brought the cinders to a fierce glow. Then he went round examining the racks of hammers and pincers. He picked up a horseshoe from a great heap stacked in a corner, enjoying its weight.

"You could 'appen do with some foot gear yourself?"

The man laughed, but gently, and Henry smiled back. Sooner or later everyone went on about his bare feet.

"I'm all right, thanks."

But the smith was serious. He went into the workshop and rummaged along the shelves.

"Now then, I thought so! See if these is any good."

He handed Henry a pair of black boots. They were grimy but instantly solid feeling, in touch with the world.

"Might just suit you, you going all the way to Carlisle."

Henry did not know what to say. He had never owned a pair of boots before.

"Try 'em on. Try 'em on," urged Torse.

The leather uppers were stiff, but Henry knew he could soften them up a bit. They weren't a bad fit.

"They're yours if you want 'em," Big Jim told Henry. "Forgot I had 'em till now."

Henry suddenly remembered the teacher. Shyly he offered his hand to the blacksmith.

"Thank ya."

Big Jim was greatly amused. "Well now, we've got manners, we have!"

Solemnly he shook Henry by the hand. "You're set up now! You can walk all the way to Kendal with them on, never you mind Carlisle."

Henry thought about it and decided not to wear his boots just yet. He tied the laces in a bow and put them round his neck so that they hung down his chest.

"I'll wear them proper when I gets used to 'em," he explained to the blacksmith.

"Of course! You do that. You'll get many a good mile out of them."

Big Jim turned and looked at the drover's bandaged face. It was evident Torse was suffering badly. "If you was wanting, 'appen I could take a squint at that old tooth of yours?"

Torse looked as if he had heard some bad news.

"No, no! Just a twinge. No bother, thank ya."

The blacksmith did not pursue it. Locals often had teeth pulled at his forge, sitting out in his old armchair. Usually he held them down with a stiff tot of whisky to help out. Still, none of his business.

"Time I was getting on. If I'm not mistaken here comes some custom."

A figure was in sight coming down the track.

Henry wished he could stay longer. But it was a bright sunlit day and the geese were beginning to wander. He whistled to Moss and the dog came running.

"Let's go."

They set off again, urging the flock forward, getting them into a steady rhythm.

It was a while before Torse spoke.

"Will you not be wearing your boots, then?"

"No," said Henry happily. "I want to think about 'em a bit. I mean, I've never had any boots afore."

Torse understood that well enough. He remembered the day he had been given his own first pair of boots, by his mother. It was not something you forgot.

"They'll walk you all the way to good fortune, will those boots!" he predicted. "Be sure they will."

Henry held them to his chest. He never wanted them to wear out.

16

Yells and Curses

Scarcely a mile further on and the good start to the day took a dismal downturn.

"It's no good, I've got to stop," moaned Torse.

He sank down alongside a beck, clutching at his jaw. The pain was growing worse.

Henry looked at the rag knotted round the drover's face. His mum would never have allowed that grubby thing. Despite the man's frequent complaints Henry felt sorry for him. He had had toothache himself.

"I'll get ya some water."

"No, no, I must rest."

They were sitting watching the flock as a man approached. When he was almost up to them the newcomer paused in the middle of the track.

"Why surely not, but it cannot be!" exclaimed the stranger. He stared from one side, and then as if that eye were not good enough, he turned his head as if to look from the other. "Bless us," he exclaimed, "Tis Torse the Goose!"

The newcomer was one of the dandiest men Henry had ever seen. He wore a black jacket, a yellow waistcoat, jodhpurs and boots, albeit everything covered in dust, yet worn with a jaunty air. A waxed moustache adorned his upper lip and his ruddy face was crowned with a black-rimmed hat. However, it was his legs that made Henry stare.

"Bandy!" exclaimed Torse. "Me old friend Bandy."

Torse forgot all his aches in a rush of talk.

Henry could see at once why the newcomer had got his name.

"Sure his legs is wide enough for a pig to be driven through, and not bump the sides," Torse informed Henry later, which was not exactly the truth.

Bandy winked hugely and produced a bottle. He explained he had already walked one lot of geese to Carlisle and was going back to Silloth for more while the season was still on them.

"Them's lovely boots, boy," said Bandy, greedily admiring the footwear round Henry's neck. Noticeably the man's own boots were peeling apart.

They sat on the bank, supping turn and turn about while Bandy recited all the latest prices of geese and cattle at the Sands market in Carlisle. And he told Henry how long ago, bless us, yes, he had seen a flock of geese walking the roads in proper boots. Real boots! Well, *nearly* real.

"Very pretty they was. Leather! Two little boot bags, one for each foot, *and* with proper draw-strings!"

Henry was not sure whether he believed him. "We'd need a lot of leather if we was to get our geese boots."

The men laughed, but Torse quickly ended in a groan.

Bandy eyed him solemnly.

"You want to be fixing that nasty tooth, old pal."

"It's not wonderful," Torse admitted.

"Get it out, I say! Get a dentist. A bad tooth is poison to

the spirit of man."

"Hah! And how would a poor drover be paying a terrible bill to get it pulled?"

"Then get the boy to do it!"

"Oh yes! The eejit wouldn't know how to begin!"

Henry glared at the drover.

Eventually Bandy rose.

"Get the boy a piece of string. He'll soon have it out!"

Bandy winked at Henry, stared longingly at his boots, then more wobbly on his feet than when he had arrived, he set off up the road, his own boots ploffing the dust as he went.

Time had flown. It was late afternoon. For once Torse had had enough. "It's no use going on any longer today, boy. We'd best be stopping here. "

He subsided to the ground, sinking deeper within his coat, distinctly unwell.

Henry took charge. An idea was beginning to form. But first he had to see to the geese. He was getting better at droving. Already he had learned how to keep the flock going on his own, and Torse seemed content to let him.

"You have a way with the geese," the drover observed, more in surprise than anything. "So you have."

Henry was recognising the birds' ways. They had preferences, just like people. It was better not to move too abruptly when near because that upset them; better still, he had learned where to stand so that he could veer them in one direction or another to where he wanted. It was a matter of turning the leaders. He caught sight of One-Eye. It was doing really well. But right now the flock needed to be safe for the night. A small field lay nearby and taking a chance, he steered the birds through the gate and shut them in.

For a while he squatted near Torse, saying nothing.

"You know, I bet I could do it," he told him at last.

"Do? Do what?"

"Like Bandy said, pull your tooth out."

At once the drover became tense. "Hah! You'll do no such thing!"

Henry did not answer. After a while he rose to his feet.

"Where are you going?"

"I'll be back."

He returned along the road they way they had come.

Three-quarters of an hour later he showed Torse two pairs of pincers. The blacksmith Big Jim had lent him two sets in case one did not fit. The drover's face filled with alarm.

"You'll not be putting those in me mouth!"

"I'm only seeing which ones'll fit!"

The blacksmith had given Henry two bits of advice. He quoted one bit now: "You'd feel a lot better after it's done."

"Oh yes, wonderful. I'll be dead!" snapped Torse.

Henry turned away. "You'll have to do it sometime."

"Oh, will I? Now don't be going off! I mean, are you sure, boy – that you can do it, I mean?"

"Course I am." And he *was* sure. Well, fairly sure. It was just a case of getting a good grip.

"Well, I isn't saying I agrees . . ."

The drover seemed to be wavering.

Henry looked solemn. He recited a bit more of Big Jim's advice.

"If you had some brandy first."

The idea did not take long to sink in.

"Jaysus, boy, you'll be a doctor you will."

The man rummaged inside his coat and pulled out a small bottle. He took a long swig. "There!" He looked at Henry hopefully. "It won't be hurting so bad now, will it?"

"Course not," said Henry, unclear whether it would or it wouldn't. He removed the vile bandage and experimentally grasped the pincers. He took hold of the drover by his shoulders.

"Ahhhhh!"

"I haven't started yet!" protested Henry.

"Well tell me, boy, when you do so's Torse is not taken by surprise. Be sure you tell me first."

"Do ya have to keep calling me *boy?*"

The drover's voice had grown a little slurred. It seemed a good moment in which to experiment.

Henry peered into the man's mouth and hurriedly drew back. It was not an inspiring sight: two rows of brown teeth with several gaps, but he could see the one that was causing the trouble. The gums were swollen round a tooth in the upper jaw.

"It's this black one."

"Black is it? Well mind you don't mangle any good ones," warned Torse worriedly. "I'm wanting to be using the others."

Henry delayed no longer; he reached in with the smaller pincers.

"I'll just try."

Before the drover could protest he got what he hoped was a good grip on the molar. He gave a trial tug.

A shriek filled the road.

"It's still in," said the boy.

"I know it is, you eejit!"

Tears ran down Torse's face.

"You jerked me arm," accused Henry.

A gruesome struggle followed. Each time he thought he had a good hold, the pincers slipped and Torse yelled. Henry determinedly locked an arm round the drover's head. He wasn't going to give up now.

It was a mess, but a moment came when he got a better grip. Holding his breath, Henry tugged hard and at last something gave. Surprised, he tumbled over backwards.

The yells of pain were worse than anything that had gone before. Blood ran from Torse's mouth as Henry sat in a heap, dazed at his success. Clamped in the pincers was the remainder of the tooth.

"Got it! I knew I could!"

It took a while for Torse to calm down.

"Ja-Jaysus, but it's gone," the drover marvelled. He mopped at his drenched face. "You've d-done it, boy!"

Skinny though he was, Henry had pulled the tooth.

The man burped loudly, and reminding himself of the antiseptic effects of alcohol he swigged the rest of the brandy and sat for a while staring at his boots. Time passed and gradually his eyes clouded until a point arrived when he tilted sideways and slowly sank down into the long grass. And there he lay asleep, the first untroubled rest in a week.

Henry was greatly relieved. He wiped the pincers and with Moss at his side he returned to the smithy. Big Jim wasn't there but he left the pincers behind the stone as the blacksmith had shown him. Feeling pleased with himself Henry returned up the road thinking he could always be a dentist if he wanted!

Torse lay in the grass snoring lustily. It was a good time to try out the boots. Feeling excited Henry pulled them on and somehow managed to tie the laces. Despite their stiffness the boots were a good fit and he walked experimentally up and down on the grass, happier than for many a day. He had no socks but it did not seem to matter. The boots felt comfortable and he guessed they would soften in time. Tearing a strip off his shirt he gave them a polish and set them down alongside Moss and himself. Tomorrow he would wear them properly, out on the road.

The night passed and when dawn came he roused Torse so they could set off with the flock before the day's heat.

The drover was surprisingly better. The bleeding had stopped. Experimentally he poked a gnarled finger into his mouth.

"There's the one," he said, counting. "And there's the two, and there's the three. But where's the next? I've lost count. How many is left?" he demanded of Henry.

Henry peered in and counted.

"Eight . . ." he announced.

"Eight! Don't be an eejit, I've got more than the eight!"

"Eight on top, and ten below, with some not there."

"Eh? Oh, *joking* are you! Well eight and ten, that's eighteen. That's good! You've done me a good job, boy. Your rewards are piling up in heaven, they are."

As wild looking as ever, he counted his teeth again until he was satisfied. For once he was grateful.

"Sure, but things are getting better. We've left the worst behind us, we have!"

Henry smirked a bit. He had shown that he knew a thing or two.

"And there you are, wearing your boots!"

"They're good," said Henry.

"Then tonight," said Torse, struck by a sudden idea. "Tonight we'll celebrate."

Henry looked inquiringly, but the drover said no more.

And so the drover and his boy set off again with the flock of cackling geese, along the path to trouble, if not immediately then certainly further on.

17

Goose Fare

The drover lunged at the nearest bird. With a swift wrench
he wrung its neck.

Henry was shocked but also impressed. Although he and
Torse were on better terms since beating off the attackers —
and the successful pulling of the tooth — the drover went on
in much the same way, sometimes crabby and bad tempered,
sometimes gloomy, and now and then bright and good
humoured. It was a loose bond between them but still it was
a bond and Henry had long ago changed his mind about
running away. He was enjoying the open road and was as
keen now as Torse to get to the market.

"You're always complaining you want to eat, boy. Well
tonight we will." Torse looked at him with a glare of
triumph. "Unless you're too high and mighty to eat with a
poor goose man!"

"I'll eat as good as you," Henry said boldly. But he felt
sorry for the dead goose. Minutes ago it had been alive and
waddling around.

They settled in another field and Torse produced a
bloodstained cord and strung the dead bird from a branch. It

hung with the blood dripping into its head where it could set and congeal while the man set about plucking it clean. "Well, don't be standing useless!" urged Torse as feathers began to whirl away. "Get sticks for a fire! It's time I learned you to cook."

The man seemed altogether different, changing at times as quickly as the weather. His special begging manner had come over him, a pleasing humble tone. He showed Henry how to strike a flint into the kindling. Henry tried and was surprised as a shower of sparks set a patch of dry moss ablaze. Torse added twigs and soon they built up a good fire.

Henry's wariness went.

Torse cleaned out the bird's innards.

"Now we gotta wrap the bird!"

First a layer of bleached grass, roughly twined so that every part of the bird was properly covered, and then a thick coating of mud, something Henry liked best. They let the fire burn for an hour before Henry took over. Following Torse's instructions he buried the corpse in the hot ashes.

"Why do you allus call me *boy?*"

Torse stared as if it were a strange question. "Well you're a boy for sure, ain't ya? Unless you're a girl that is!"

"Cumberland folk say *lad*. We get called *lad* in Cumberland."

"Do you now! Well I'll eat my boots! A drover's lad! Just keep that fire going or there'll be trouble, lad or no lad."

Night came before they broke open the clay surrounding the goose. A tantalising smell assailed them and Henry gave in to hunger. Ravenous and groggy, he tugged at a leg, gulping it down. Torse was as quick. It was good and savoury with plenty to go round. Even Moss got a piece.

The food had a good effect on Torse.

"So, just the one brother has you?"

He lay inside his coat, nursing his aches, but thinking for the first time since leaving Silloth that maybe he had been too hard on Henry.

"He's called Ruben," said Henry. "But he's not as big as me."

"Well, that's nothing. I have eleven brothers."

"Eleven?" said Henry disbelievingly. He stuck his head up out of the ditch.

"Well, not eleven exactly, 'cause four did go and die when they was born, so they did, not liking what they found."

"Well that still leaves seven."

"Nine! With me, nine. And if we count me half-brother Dan, ten. And I'm the only one who's done good, with Liam the worst of us. Dozy that he is."

Henry couldn't work out Torse's sums, but he let it go. He remembered something else. "You said he hit a copper, then you said he broke a leg."

"Yes, well . . . he thumped that interfering Constable Stoppers right enough! We was only carrying a poor dead sheep what we found lying in the road. And why not? But it's not sounding so good telling that to the Garda."

Come morning, they set off early with the geese and for the first time in days Henry was not hungry. They knocked at doors as they went, selling a dozen birds here, three or four there, or sometimes just the one. In this way they reached the outskirts of Carlisle a few days later and padded along the cobbled streets to the old *Fox and Hounds* in Rickergate. The geese cackled loudly as they were driven into a lane behind the inn where they were boxed in behind the rails of a makeshift pen. Their timing was perfect. The market was the next morning. They had three hundred and sixty-five birds left. To Henry it seemed an enormous number to try to sell in one day. Time would show if they succeeded.

18

Battling Drovers

A roar of voices filled the lane as the drover slipped and crashed to the cobbles. Henry was at the front of the throng, his face bright with excitement.

"On your feet, Ryan! On your feet!"

"Finish him Paddy!"

Boos and jeers mingled with encouraging yells. A fortune in bets had been laid out. Every drover in Carlisle seemed to be in the crowded lane cheering the boxers.

Never had Henry seen such a fight! Both men stood stripped to the waist hammering one another with bared knuckles. The fight might have been taking place in Ireland itself, though it wasn't, for in all Carlisle *The Fox and Hounds* was a favourite spot with the Irish. The noisy circle of drovers crowding the lane was Irish to the core.

Henry groaned as a gnarled fist smacked noisily into a man's face. The boxer tumbled into the spectators, landing almost at Henry's feet.

Despairing shouts sounded. "Get on with it, Paddy!"

Paddy was given no choice. Forceful hands got him to his feet and pushed him back into the middle.

"Finish him! Finish him!"

Scarcely an hour had passed since Henry and Torse had landed in the heart of the smoky city and had lodged the geese. Moss was hitched to a rail and left to keep watch over them as the landlord came and announced the contest, and a rush of betting began.

The fight was fair but it could not last. For several more frantic minutes Henry watched with mixed feelings. He found himself feeling sorry for Paddy as he lost the advantage, and then he felt sorry for Ryan as he was knocked flying. The pace was killing and the movements of both men began to grow sluggish.

The impasse did not please the crowd. The jeers grew noisier.

"Get on with it you eejits!"

But they couldn't. Eighteen minutes into the fight, with no clear winner, both men sweaty and gasping came to an exhausted standstill. They sagged into one another's arms.

Sarcastic boos greeted this wicked letdown.

Abruptly the landlord pushed past Henry into the circle.

"Will I settle it, lads?" he cried out. "Is it over?"

Henry was surprised. The appeal was not directed at the boxers, but at the crowd.

"Settle it, John. Settle it!"

"And no fighting afterwards." His generous scowl broke into a broad grin. "Well, not much!"

Laughter and a sea of waving betting slips greeted him.

"Then I'll decide it. 'Tis the push that will finish it!"

Without further warning the landlord rammed his bulky body shoulder-first into the exhausted contestants. Everybody except Henry seemed to know it had been coming, but it was still a shock. Paddy staggered several steps yet somehow managed to keep his balance and it was Ryan who was the unlucky one and crashed to the ground.

An excited roar filled the yard.

The landlord did not wait. He grabbed at the swaying Paddy and held up an arm. "I declare Paddy O'Flynn the winner!"

Lusty boos mingled with cheers. Loosing punters angrily waved a sea of betting slips. For a scaring moment Henry thought the whole place was going to turn into one big fight. He caught Torse's glance but the drover shook his head.

The landlord was aware of the risk and knew his customers well. "'Tis a free pint of beer for the winners," he shouted loudly. And then still louder: "And a half-pint for the losers, you idle devils!'"

Boos turned to cheers. The man had taken no chances. In any case, a fat wodge of the lost betting would land in his own pocket.

Henry hung around with the crowd excitedly hoping for more. "Was they fighting for money, mister?" he demanded of a drover.

The man took a pipe out of his mouth and laughed. He was broad shouldered with a bushy beard. His droving smock came almost to the ground. "For sure, yes, young fella!" His eyes shone. "That is to say, after a manner of speaking they was. They was fighting 'cause Ryan tried to push in on Paddy's cattle deal, so he did. And they was fighting 'cause they're Irish! You must know Irish drovers is mad for a good fight!"

"So are our farmers," said Henry boldly.

"Oh yes, and who told you such a thing as that?"

Henry stared back. "Cumberland farmers fight as good as

any Irishman," he bragged.

"Is that so?"

The drover looked searchingly into Henry's face. "And you are a fighting man yourself, then?"

"Course I am! I'm always winning fights."

"Well now, isn't that interesting. Sure now, I can see we mustn't miss a chance like this!"

The drover knocked out his pipe and his voice rose as he seized Henry by the collar. To the boy's alarm, he was thrust bodily out into the circle of men.

"Here lads! Here's another fighter! This young Cumberland master is wanting to take on the best of the Irish!"

"Lemme go," yelled Henry, struggling to break free. "Lemme go."

Laughter filled the lane.

"Ten rounds and no quarter given – unless, that is, you has perhaps changed your mind?"

"I has!" yelled Henry. "I has!"

The man towed him back. "There now," he said, and his voice dropped. "I'll tell you what lad, when you've grown a bit stronger we'll have you back to fight the best drover from all Ireland. Now how's that?"

The man half grinned. Henry hesitated then, despite his fright, he found himself grinning back.

"Make sure you don't be forgetting now!"

Henry ducked clear, trembling at his lucky escape.

Knowing smirks were directed his way.

"And what was that about?" It was Torse. "Turning into a no-good boxer, are you! And I thought I was teaching you to be a good Irish drover."

The two of them moved away, Henry telling how it had happened.

Torse said: "That's a good man, you met, that is. That's Donal O'Brian, and very rich he is with the money. I'd be terrible wealthy meself if I had half his pennies, I would."

"He don't look rich," said Henry. The man had looked almost shabby.

"Don't go judging a man by his clothes," said Torse hitching his voluminous coat tighter round him.

Henry grinned at that.

Together they returned to the pen. It was time to keep a watch on the geese before the market started in the morning.

A figure in the crowd watched them go. Had they noticed him they would have been more on their guard.

19

Knife Scare

Torse pushed Henry down alongside a line of railings.

Overhead a gas lamp popped and spluttered, its rays lighting a timber den which Torse said was the Dugout. It looked a bit like the Doss, thought Henry, and a good place to shelter but the drover waved him to stay out where he was.

"Don't you fall asleep, boy! There's some round here who'd pinch every bird we've got given the chance."

"Who are they?"

"Never you mind!"

The drover turned away.

"Where are you going?"

"Business, boy. Man's business."

"Let me come. Why can't I come?"

He suddenly did not want to stay with the geese. Despite the gas lamp the place seemed unfriendly.

"Listen will you! Your job's to watch the birds. Keep that dog where I've set him and you stay quiet!"

"Why can't Moss be here with me?"

The dog was tethered on the opposite side of the pen

looking downcast.

"Because he'll stop anyone getting past on his side. Now shut up!"

The drover moved off and disappeared into the back door of the *Fox and Hounds*.

Henry waited several minutes then picked his way through the geese and gave Moss a piece of biscuit. For a while he stayed alongside but a door kept opening and closing, splashing the yard with light and though he felt bad at leaving Moss he went back to his place by the rails.

Miserably he sank down. The journey was nearly over, this part anyway. But what could he do now? In a few days they would return to Silloth and he was beginning to feel that he did not want to. Not yet. What if he didn't go home at all? Somehow he felt he was a different person from that first nervous night in the Doss. It was not cold, yet for some reason he shivered. Still thirteen, but at times he felt older.

Noises spilled into the night. A piano, shouts and talking, a wavering voice declaring *Rose Marie I Love You*. There were shrieks of laughter; Henry nodded sleepily. The geese filled the pen in a fidgeting patch.

He woke up sharply. Someone had coughed. How long had he dozed? A figure staggered past and he realised it was Torse. The drover stumbled in the blackness, grumbling because the gas lamp had gone out. Wading through the protesting geese, the man sank into a corner of the pen and gradually turned into a snoring heap.

Later a clock sounded distantly and Henry was startled by the sound of a bullock drinking noisily at a trough somewhere behind him. The animal's slurping masked the steps of the approaching man. Then it happened. A muscular arm locked round his throat.

He tried to yell but couldn't. He couldn't breathe. Terrified, he found himself being hoisted up backwards like a sack and dragged over the top of the rail.

"Just the one I's wanting to meet!" snarled Jergo. A knife blade glinted. "There's a little job I's got for you."

"Ow! Lemme go!"

"Quiet!"

The point of the knife jabbed sharply against Henry's windpipe.

"Listen, boy, listen carefully!" Jergo's voice was low and harsh. "What you do next you'd better do well. You is going to cross the yard, see, and you is going to slide your clever little hands inside the old fool's coat. And you is going to find his money pouch, and you is going to bring it to me."

"I can't!" gasped Henry, shaking with fright. "He'll kill me!"

"Oh yes you can, you skinny runt! And I'll show you why."

The man forced Henry's palm down onto the top of the metal rail. A moment later he set the blade of his knife across the back of Henry's knuckles. It felt deadly cold and sharp.

"You feel that steel, eh? Well, you get me his pouch or we'll saw your little fingers off, one by one, till there's only your thumbs left and once they're off then we drops 'em all down the pee hole. Now just think on that!"

Had Henry not seen Jergo beating Torse he might not have believed him. But he knew the man could easily carry out his threat.

"Now do it! And don't think to go a-running, because I'll hunt you down like a dog!"

Jergo thrust him through a gap in the railings.

Henry could see no way to escape. Trembling, he pushed

through the birds, hesitated and seeing there was no other choice he sank down beside Torse.

The drover was snoring heavily.

"Do it!" hissed Jergo.

Henry lifted a flap of the coat and felt inside. A shiver went through him, and then unexpectedly one of sudden hope as his hand closed on a smooth wooden handle.

Jergo's husky voice sounded: "You got it boy? Has you got it?"

Before Henry could answer, a door opened and light lanced across the yard. Jergo turned swiftly as a figure emerged, and after a moment a man began to pee against a wall. The distraction gave Henry time to get back across to the gap.

"It's here," he said, closing in.

But it wasn't a purse. He swung the shillelagh up from behind him and brought it crashing down on the man's shoulder. Jergo gave an agonised cry. Without waiting, Henry tried a second blow and by a fluke caught the tramp where it hurt most, on the elbow. Yelling with pain, Jergo dropped his knife and buckled over.

"What's all this?"

The man had come across from the wall.

"Why, 'tis the young boxer."

The bearded drover, Donal O'Brian, loomed over them. "And who is this?"

"It's Jergo," said Henry, white faced. And then: "He was going to stab me."

More men appeared. Among them a stupefied looking Torse. Henry blurted out about Jergo's attack and the shillelagh and everything.

"The boy's lying!" blustered Jergo trying to move away.

"I'm not!" cried Henry. "See, *there's* his knife!"

The blade lay gleaming on the cobbles.

The onlookers needed no more proof. Excited men seized the tramp. Yelling loudly, he was frog-marched away.

"After me pouch, was he?"

Anxiously Torse checked the drawstring.

"He nearly got it," said Henry.

O'Brian said: "I'm thinking you have a good lad here."

Torse nodded vigorously and then, knowing he was being watched, he patted Henry on the top of his head. "I told you, boy, didn't I, how me shillelagh would be the saving of us! I told you I did."

It was as near as the befuddled Torse got to being generous.

20

The Great Sands Market

Only seven o'clock in the morning and already the Great Sands Market by the River Eden was seething.

Henry was struggling to keep the geese together. Such excitement! Such noise! Cattle were everywhere, arriving in a rush, bellowing, churning cinders, wide-eyed and scatty, the black Irish bullocks liveliest of the lot as they charged down the lines of pens. Alarmed, the geese tried to escape but each time were foiled. Henry and Moss got there before them.

"Jipe, jipe, jipe!"

The morning was filled with drovers' cries. They were a rough gang, energetic and ragged, hard faced and cursing, yet they knew their job and rarely did the cattle go wrong. It was an old market. All knew how it worked.

A giant of a man shouted at Henry. "Stand clear! Stand clear!" He waved at him to move the geese aside.

But Henry stood his ground.

"The goose paddock, boy! Into the paddock!" cried Torse.

Henry turned the geese into a bare earth paddock.

"Don't let 'em in with the others!" yelled the drover. Wilder than ever, his coat flapping, he hopped about excitedly.

A second flock was inside the paddock. Henry never faltered. He steered the geese into a side pen and dragged the gate shut. He got back his breath.

"Can I sell 'em too?" he asked.

Torse screwed up his face. "You?"

"I know how. I've sold geese before."

"Two," said the drover. "You sold two."

"Well, I did all right."

"Don't go putting no money in your pocket!"

"Course I won't!"

"Two shillings a time! But you give me the money right away."

"I know what to do!"

Seven twenty-nine on a bright morning, their timing was good. Henry was excited. He could hardly believe they were there.

But Torse could believe it. The drover was calmer now and rubbing his hands in anticipation. The main market had not yet started, but already a stocky farmer's wife was peering into the goose pen.

"Watch me boy, and be learning!" he hissed.

Eagerly he hurried forward.

"Here you are, missis! Lovely fresh geese. Good fatteners. All the way from the green fields of Ireland to grace your Christmas table!"

The woman laughed. "Fresh! They look as if they need a good feed to me!"

Torse was on top form. "Set 'em to eat in the golden stubble, tell 'em how beautiful they are, and they'll be fat as pigs by Christmas," he assured her.

"Is that so! And how much is you wanting for that 'un?"

She had picked out one of the sturdiest.

Torse glanced knowingly at Henry. "Only two shillings and one sixpence. Cheap at the price!"

"I'll give you one and six and nowt more."

Torse was not put off. "I couldn't, missis. But make it two bob, and it's yours – with a handsome bit of string thrown in to lead it away!"

The woman left, still laughing, the goose on a string, two shillings paid.

Henry grinned at Torse's success. The first sale of the day. And moments later a delighted Henry made his own first sale. Fat as a pig by Christmas, he affirmed. Honest, they would find no better Irish geese anywhere.

Two good shillings landed in his hand.

From this moment they never stopped selling as droves of people began to arrive. The birds went in ones and twos at first, but then two brothers bought sixty and drove them away in a cackling gaggle, and almost immediately Henry sold twenty to a butcher.

By quarter to eleven Henry did a quick count and was astonished to find that a hundred and thirty eight geese had gone already. Canny housewives and farmers looked into the other pens before returning to Torse and Henry and buying off them. Theirs were quite the best geese there.

The rush went on. Henry hadn't a moment free, catching birds as they were pointed out, sometimes tying a string round their necks so their new owners could walk them away.

And quite suddenly they were down to the last batch. Torse's money pouch was heavy with coins.

"We've done well, boy. We've done well."`

Henry realised with a pang of regret that soon his long trek to the Great Sands Market would be over. It was time he was paid. Reluctantly he approached Torse.

The drover gave him a wild-eyed look at the mention of money. His jovial manner changed to one of caution.

"Sure, we must settle up we must . . ."

"Aye, well," said Henry. It had taken a big effort to mention it.

Torse stared hard.

"It'll be two weeks, at a shilling a week." But as the words did not seem to register, he added: "For walking the geese."

"*Two shillings?*" said Torse in disbelief. "You'll not be getting anny two shillings from me, boy! You can think again on that one!"

21

Diddled!

The Great Sands market place suddenly lost its magic.

Henry faltered. The drover's face had developed a hard look.

"But you told me I'd get a shilling a week!" said Henry. "*And* you said you owes me."

Torse looked uncomfortable. "That's right! That's right it is. Torse owes you! And where would a poor drover like meself be finding two whole shillings?"

Henry pointed at Torse's coat. "In there, you've lots!"

"Ah, me coat." The man's eyes narrowed. "Me coat is me home, boy, you know that. Me a-sleeping in it, minding the geese! But there's not a penny in me coat I can call me own, except to pay the poor famished divils back home in Ireland who fed the birds with every crumb they had."

Henry glared in disbelief. "Then I'll tell folk how you're a rotten twister! And how you haven't paid my wages!"

"A twister! Oh! That's a wicked thing to be saying! And all the free lessons I've given you a-droving. *Free*, they was! The art of the road! Boy – it's *you* who owes *me!*"

"I don't! Me wages was for me mother. You wait till you meet Nathan!"

Torse's face betrayed a trace of anxiety. He had forgotten about Nathan. He changed direction. "Two shillings, is it? All right, then, as you are so clever."

His voice turned sarcastic. "I'll give you your *earnings*. See if I don't. And Silloth won't see no more of me because I'll not be back to Silloth!"

A wave of cackling arose as he plunged in among the birds. When he returned he was dangling a lean looking goose. Henry recognised it immediately.

"Here's your earnings," said the drover. "And don't be saying I aren't gen'rous. This fine bird will fetch two shillings of anybody's money."

"It won't," said Henry angrily. "It's the limping one."

"Listen, boy! This is Carlisle. Use your wits! Town people is no good with the money, every drover knows it! Now that's learning you something useful, that is."

He dangled the struggling creature before Henry.

"Take it, boy, tis all you're getting."

Henry shook his head. "It's only got one eye. It's the bird I saved."

"And what of it? This fine goose will be the making of your fortune."

The man slipped a string noose round the bird's neck and thrust the end at him.

"Tis the goose or nothing."

Unwillingly Henry took hold of the string.

"Now you be telling your ole Ma how I've looked after you," said Torse, as if the matter were settled.

"I'll not! I'll tell her you're a rotten twister!"

Too late Henry remembered the warning long ago at the

Doss. He had been diddled. Worse he had no money. Not even a penny. All he had was a one-eyed goose and a dog, hungry like himself.

22

Torse is Off

Two hours more and the market place was almost empty.

Torse muttered for a second time. "Must be getting off now, boy . . . getting on me way."

He spoke hesitantly. Partings meant little to the man. But of the lads who had walked with him droving he had to admit to himself that Henry had been the best. Not everyone could pull out a tooth just like that.

"Aye," said Henry worriedly. He stood at the edge of the market place the goose on one side and Moss the other. So Torse was not going to walk back to Silloth after all. He was going on without him.

"Get the goose sold," said the drover reassuringly, "and you'll be home in no time."

Henry stared down. His boots were muddy and his feet ached. Upset though he was at being diddled, the thought of Torse leaving filled him with dismay. He knew he was going to miss the little man even if he was a cheat. Anything was better than going back to Nathan.

"Can't I go with you a bit – I mean, just to Brampton?

I'll do it for nowt."

Torse shook his head. With the last fifty geese sold to another flock master, he had got himself a job helping to walk the man's birds on to the next little town. Several days' good pay.

"The fella's got all the help he wants. Annyway, you've your own goose to look after."

It was true. The bird stood pathetically at Henry's side, tethered by the string. In one way Henry was glad to have it, but he knew he would have to sell it so he could pay Nathan − if he did decide to pay him. Perhaps he wouldn't.

"Only one eye," he said, reminding himself, rather than saying anything new.

"Don't I keep telling ya, that makes no difference! Once the bird is sitting inside a good hot oven it will taste as good as anny . . . And now I see 'em!"

Beyond the pens a mass of geese was in sight. Several hundred birds were gathering in a white rippling patch. Shouts sounded as a distant figure saw Torse and waved.

Hurriedly the drover brought out the last of his flock.

"Good birds, every one. Good Irish birds."

He waved his shillelagh to start them moving.

"See you boy."

Henry nodded wretchedly.

"See ya."

He held Moss by the scruff of his neck and watched the last of their geese move away and join up with the giant flock. Nothing more happened for a while, then amid cackling and shouts the great concourse started to move towards the bridge over the River Eden and take the road to Brampton.

Henry felt let down. Perhaps he ought to get on his own

way, though it would be better to sell the goose first. The crowds had gone but he knew he ought to try.

For a long time he waited by the empty pen and at last it seemed his luck was in for a man paused.

"What's this, eh? Pinched yourself a goose, has ya?"

He looked like a labourer.

Henry flushed. "It's not pinched. It's for sale. And I've earned it."

"Oh, aye."

The man eyed the bird sharply.

"Lame, is it?"

"That don't matter," said Henry. "Put it on good stubble and it'll fatten up. It's a good Irish bird."

The man examined Henry's face, saw the boy's thinness. "A shilling, I'll give ya a shilling."

He made it sound like a favour.

"Two," said Henry nervously, and then, remembering Torse. "It's worth *two* good shillings."

"Hah! You'll have a job getting two bob for a skinny un like this!"

Henry could feel the sale slipping away. Perhaps he ought to take the shilling.

"Tell you what . . ." The man moved closer and a whiff of bad breath hit Henry's face. "I'll give you one and tuppence!"

Henry pulled back. "I've changed me mind," he said.

He didn't like this man.

"What?"

"It's not for sale. I'm going to keep it."

The man swore as Henry towed the bird clear. He would find another customer.

He turned to the town. Somehow the tightly clustered

buildings and streets seemed less welcoming than yesterday. With the goose and Moss at his heels he retraced his steps to *The Fox and Hounds*. He was lucky, the lane was empty and the three retreated into the Dugout, hungry but out of sight.

Men came and went during the night but no one suspected he was there. The Dugout was a real stink hole, peed in, and at daylight he was glad to get out and go back into the town centre.

A horse and cart clattered past and the noise of the wheels set the goose off in a frightened flap. Faces turned to look as Henry grabbed up the bird and belted across the cobbles to the safety of a pavement. He hurried up a narrow street and paused breathless outside a stone building.

"You're a blithering nuisance!" he said, setting the bird down. The morning seemed beset with problems. And another came.

Three boys clattered into sight kicking a ball.

"Wa-hey lads, look at this!"

They clustered round.

"Goosy, goosy on a string! Pinched it, 'ave ya?"

"No I hasn't," snapped Henry. Why did folk keep saying that! "I've earned it."

"Ohhhh, *earned* it!" The boss boy had small eyes and a pudgy face. He saw Henry as an easy target. "Well feathers is meant for plucking, they is."

He grabbed at the goose's tail tuft and gave it a hard tug. A yell of pain sounded as a beak stabbed him on the nose.

"Ouch! Ow!"

At the same time Moss grabbed the boy round an ankle.

"Gerroff! You devil! Gerroff!"

The boys kicked out, driving Moss back. Henry looked up and down the road, desperate for help. There was no one in sight. He backed into a doorway prepared to fight.

"I'll kill that dog, you skinbag!" yelled the boss boy. "And yer goose with it!"

He might easily have tried except for a quirk of luck. As they closed in, the heavy wooden door at Henry's back took him by surprise, yielding unexpectedly on big hinges. With a yell he pitched back through the opening, the goose tumbling in with him.

23

Goodbye to the Goose

He landed on a stone floor, the goose flapping about him in an excited flurry of wings. The door swung and clicked shut but his relief was short-lived. Moss was still on the outside.

He was in a high-roofed market hall with people busily loading stalls.

"Hello! Just dropped in, have you?"

A stocky woman with a jolly face was beside him. She wore a blue and white striped apron and a straw hat. "Bought yourself a nice goose for Christmas?"

She grinned as she heaped leeks onto a table.

"I haven't bought it," said Henry. "It – it's for sale – but I've just lost me dog . . ."

The woman seemed only to have half-heard.

"Oh, for sale is it?"

She peered at the goose, and then stared along the lines of stalls. Her expression softened. "You need the outside market for that, petal," she said gently. "I mean we don't sell much live stuff just here, not *officially* that is. What with old Fisher, the market inspector . . ."

Henry was desperate to go and look for Moss, but he had the goose as well.

The woman hesitated, took in his skinny figure. "Tell you what, put your bird below my stall and we can try selling it. So long as it's done nice and quiet."

Her smile was warm and generous. Encouraged, Henry nodded.

"It was my pay. The goose – I got it for droving."

"Did you now! Well feed it up a bit and it'll make a fine oven bird."

"But I've lost my dog."

He explained what had happened and this time she caught on and waved him to stop.

"Goodness,. You must hurry! Help find a spot for the bird then off you go and look."

They settled the goose on a piece of sacking below the leeks. Henry tied the string round a bench leg and the bird sat calmly enough.

"From Silloth, are you? I went to Silloth on me 'olidays once! Windy it was, though a bonny place . . ."

And to a customer: "Yes, missis, lovely leeks, grown 'em meself!"

Henry raced out through the main entrance into the street. Warily he turned into the side road and saw the doorway. The boys were no longer there – neither was Moss.

For half an hour he trailed up and down the town centre searching. It wasn't just the dog; he knew he had to get back to the goose.

The market hall was filling with shoppers. Mrs Atkinson, for so she introduced herself, was busy.

"He'll turn up," she told him reassuringly. "They usually

do. I never knew a dog that didn't turn up at meal times."

"Can I help ya?" Henry volunteered.

He loaded more carrots from a reserve sack. It gave him something else to think about.

"Got a new assistant, have we!" said a sharp voice. It was Fisher, the market inspector. He passed with a nod, intent on another matter.

Mrs Atkinson stared after him.

"We need to be selling your bird."

Henry nodded hopefully.

"Leave it to me, petal."

The gabble of voices rose. By eleven o'clock the hall was crowded with shoppers. Twice women loaded with shopping bags looked at the goose but they made no offers. Then someone stopped.

"And how much is that un, then?"

A rough looking man eyed the bird.

Henry glanced at Mrs Atkinson and caught her nod.

"Two shillings," he said firmly.

"Nay." The man looked bleak. "I's only wanting the goose; not you with it. I'll give you a shillin. "

An indignant Mrs Atkinson took over. "Two shillings is cheap in anybody's money. An Irish goose, you won't buy better!"

The man shook his head and moved away.

"A shilling! The old misery. Don't worry petal, there's plenty more folk here yet."

Henry helped by wrapping customers' vegetables, and a grateful Mrs Atkinson brewed two mugs of tea. In between sales she heard how he had slept in the Dugout, and Moss had been outside the market when he had fallen through the door.

"Off you go and have another look," advised Mrs Atkinson.

For fifty minutes he trailed through the town once more, but still without success.

Afternoon came. Just a few carrots were left. Dismally Henry started to clear them away. No one had bought the goose and in a way he was glad. Losing Moss was bad enough. If the goose went it would feel worse.

The stall keeper sighed and rummaged for her coat. She was bothered about the bird and wondering what to say when a middle-aged woman loaded with shopping stopped by.

Mrs Atkinson's face lit up. "Why, it's Mrs Liddle. I asked meself was you in town today, and here you are."

The newcomer was badly out of breath. "Gone and forgot the carrots . . . and Mr Liddle out at the cart when I need him."

"Nay, I've carrots left. Had a real rush, but I've had a bit of extra help from young Henry here. Nice and handy he's been."

"Pleased to meet you."

"Henry's walked all the way from Silloth to sell his goose."

"Oh aye, from Silloth?" Mrs Liddle glanced down at the bird. "I used to take me holidays in Silloth. Is this un to sell, then?"

"It's for Christmas fattening," explained Henry. "But it won't be no good if it doesn't get on some good stubble first."

The woman laughed. "Our farm's plenty of that! And how much was you asking?"

Nervously Henry told her two shillings and a moment

later the money landed in his palm.

"Well isn't that just grand!" said Mrs Atkinson. She smiled cheerfully. "It'll make a good Christmas dinner that will."

"It will if I get this lot back to me husband," said Mrs Liddle.

"Can I help?" said Henry.

Which is how he found himself carrying the goose as he followed the farmer's wife through the stalls. Proudly he told her about the journey with the flock, and how he had pulled out Torse's tooth, and he was thinking he might go home but wasn't sure. And now he had lost his dog and he had searched everywhere.

Mrs Liddle puffed and panted, saying, "Well I never. He'll turn up. Dogs usually do," by which time they reached a crowded street and struggled along it until they found the right pony and cart where Mr Liddle was waiting.

"This is Henry," the woman told him. "He's walked all the way from Silloth."

The farmer did not smile, but he did not look unfriendly either. "That's a long way for a young man to be walking. And whose is the goose?"

Henry clutched the bird tighter. Dismally he realised he was about to part with it. "It's mine. − I mean I've sold it your missis."

"I thought it would do us for Christmas," said Mrs Liddle. "Fattened up, instead of a turkey."

The farmer nodded. "Aye, well it can travel in the old box."

"I'd better get back and help Mrs Atkinson," said Henry. He handed the bird over.

"You carry on, my lad. She's always one for being busy."

Mrs Liddle seemed about to say more but her husband got

her to hold open a crate while he pushed the goose in. Henry left, sorry the bird had gone.

Mrs Atkinson's stall stood empty. Dejectedly he went outside and a pang of loneliness crept over him. He sat down at the kerb edge. For the first time in days he didn't know where he was going any more. Fleetingly he had thought to stop in Carlisle, but now he was not sure. Nor was he sure about going home to face Nathan. Without the flock to look after he could be back in Silloth within days but did he really want to? First he must find Moss. Perhaps at the police station.

"And why are you looking so glum, young man?"

A woman had spoken. He had not heard the pony and cart approach. It was Mr and Mrs Liddle.

24

A Darraker

Mrs Liddle looked down. "Well now, if it's not a rude question, where would a young man like you be a-sleeping tonight?"

Henry scrambled to his feet and for a moment was unable to answer. He had not thought that far ahead.

"It called the Dugout...." He said at last.

"That'll be at the old *Fox and Hounds*" said Mr. Liddle, "In Rickergate.'

Mrs Liddle smiled. "Nay, I thought you was telling me you was going back home, like."

"Oh, I am," said Henry, flushing. "I'm going soon."

She waved at the cart. "Well get yourself up here. We're taking the same road – just short of Fingland anyway and that'll knock a few miles off your journey."

Fingland. Henry remembered Fingland well. There was something good about the name, something he liked.

"I can't. I've lost me dog."

For the second time that day he explained what had happened.

Mr Liddle said: "So where did he live?"

Henry looked miserable. "Don't know. Back in Silloth . . . but he must have come from a farm."

And then suddenly he knew where Moss would be.

"We'll take you," said Mr Liddle. "No, no, get up here with us. It's not far out of our way."

"I'm just guessing," said Henry.

The cart turned along Rickergate to *The Fox and Hounds.* Henry hurried into the lane and there was Moss lying in the Dugout entrance, his head flat to the ground.

It was a joyful reunion. In a moment the dog was bouncing round and round.

"Good boy!" said Henry.

"A sheepdog," said Mr Liddle approvingly. "Well now, we'll have to make space for him!"

Henry climbed up into the cart and with Moss at his feet he abandoned thoughts of finding a job in Carlisle. The cart was fully laden but the fell pony was strong and soon it was picking its way along cobbled streets to the town's outskirts.

As they went he told the Liddles about his droving adventures, and in turn, Mr Liddle remembered how he had driven a boisterous cow to market for his father, and it had run away and landed inside a glasshouse full of tomatoes. "Whoever bought that 'un got tomato soup with it!"

Henry told how bullocks fresh in from Ireland had done the same. Well, nearly the same. One had belted out of Silloth dockyard and raced down the road past their house. "A big un got right into a sweet shop and sat on a counter!"

"Well I never!"

"Honest! Well – sort of. Perhaps it weren't *sitting*, but the counter was all busted."

More seriously, he told them of Ruben, and how his mother washed clothes for a living, and how long he had been away from home. He mentioned Nathan, but only briefly.

They plodded on past fields and farms and as the cart began to cover the miles Henry fell silent and wondered if he was being foolish. His future seemed so uncertain. All he knew was he did not want Nathan to find him another job. He would find his own jobs.

Mr Liddle said: "Seems to me a hard working droving lad like yourself might want to rest up a bit? All your walking! I mean, if you wanted, you and the dog could stop at our spot for a day or two."

The farmer looked at his wife.

She nodded approvingly. "Aye, we've plenty of space. There's a place in the loft."

Cautiously Mr Liddle added: "But only if you is wanting."

Henry could hardly believe his luck. At once he knew he wanted to accept. There was nothing he would like better, he told them. Just for a day or two, if that would be all right? And how could he thank them?

It was agreed.

Come dusk, the cart bumped down a track and halted in front of a small farmhouse. A painted wooden sign told them they were at Ploughrigg. Fingland proper was a bit further on.

"Put the bird in a pen while I get supper," said Mrs Liddle. "And I'll see what I can find for the dog."

Moss was already exploring the farmyard.

The farmer lit an oil lamp and rubbed down the pony in the byre and gave it a feed. Then he helped Henry carry the goose box to an old hen run. The run was in a bad state, though the wooden hut at one end seemed secure. Henry seized the bird and put it inside with a bowl of water and a scoop of grain.

"We'll fettle it up proper tomorrow," said the farmer.

"Perhaps it will lay some eggs," said Henry.

"Aye, but not yet. Bit too cold. I mind a time we used to hatch geese in our kitchen under the table where it was warm! Me dad set the goose's eggs in a straw nest under it."

"Didn't you tread on 'em?"

"Nay. But when I was little I was terrified! Used to peck me knees! It took years afore I got keen about geese."

Henry grinned. He could tell already he liked this farmer.

"Now let's be having supper and afterwards we'll find a warm spot in the barn for the dog."

Tattie pot stew with black pudding slices: Henry ate as if he were starving. Steamed jam sponge pudding covered in custard: he was full to bursting! At bedtime he climbed up into the loft feeling as if he would never need to eat again. What a day! He flopped into the bed happier than for a long time. A real bed with sheets, and no need to look for frogs. Not for a night or two anyway.

All morning Henry hammered and sawed. The farm was sandstone built with blue slate roofs and from one building or another he rummaged out nails and pieces of wood, as well as a real find, half a roll of chicken wire left in a corner. By noon he had repaired the hen run.

"That's a grand job," said Mr Liddle approvingly. "It'll keep yon fox out for sure."

Henry was pleased. "I like mending things."

The farmer sat on an upended tub. "You could make a living being a darraker you could, given a bit more experience."

Henry had never heard of a darraker.

"He's a kind of handy man. Does repairs and such. Fixes slates and stops gaps in walls, owt really. But why don't you let the bird out into the run?"

The goose liked the open space. It padded up and down, staring at them through the wire.

"Only one eye," explained Henry.

"So it has."

"But it sees a lot. It knows what's going on."

"Aye. It's bright enough. Give it a day or two and we'll let it out round the yard. It'll soon start fattening up."

And then, more quietly: "I'm thinking, me lad, you was fonder of this bird than you knows."

Henry, unsure what to say, said nothing.

Two days sped by. The Liddles found him odd jobs, chopping kindling, collecting the hen eggs, knocking down a broken fence. Each day end he was tired and glad to sit at the evening meal. He knew he would be sorry when he left.

The third morning came.

"Well?" said Mr Liddle, breakfast over. His wife set down the tea pot. "Nay, you ask him, Ted."

"Aye. Well. You'll have seen me and Mary doesn't do much farming now. Getting on like. We wonders how you'd fancy stopping on a bit, for a wage, of course, a proper job. We could use a likely lad."

Henry was surprised, and at the same time excited. "A sort of darraker?"

"Aye, a bit like that. Anyway, until you think to go home."

"But there's Moss."

Mr Liddle laughed. "He seems to have made himself at home already."

Moss lay stretched out in front of the fire trying not to be noticed.

His dog . . . and the goose. Henry did not speak for a moment but his thoughts were racing. Mostly it was the goose. A wild idea came, but dare he ask?

"It's the goose," he explained. "I mean, if I stayed on, worked proper for you and saved me pay w–would you sell it back? I mean, not kill it at Christmas?"

He felt silly. Who had ever heard of buying back a goose he'd just sold?

Mr Liddle stopped himself from smiling. Mary Liddle spoke first. "We doesn't really need us a goose for our Christmas dinner, does we Ted? I mean they can be a bit fatty."

The farmer did not immediately mention the goose but talked instead about Henry's wages. A pound a month, plus his board and keep, or a full £6 10 shillings if he stayed for the proper half-year hiring term. It was generous payment.

Henry's mind raced. Five shillings a week!

"But the goose?"

"Aye, well, come Christmas I guess we'll be able to struggle along with a turkey. Mind you, if yon fox gets your goose it'll be on your own head!"

"It won't," vowed Henry. "I promise. Moss will guard it."

For the moment going home was put aside. There was plenty to do where he was.

Mr Liddle turned to the door. "What the devil's that?"

A clatter of hooves sounded outside. The farmer and Henry hurried out.

A bullock had arrived at a fast run, snorting militantly. Hemmed in by buildings, it paused in the middle of the yard.

Ted Liddle called: "Henry! Stand still, will you, just where you are? That's it!"

The farmer moved to head it off.

Henry stretched out his arms.

"Steady, now, steady . . ."

The farmer's voice was warm and strong and safe. He closed in slowly and while the bullock stood as if to charge off again, he reached forward and grasped hold of it's horns. At once it tried to swing away, but the farmer held fast.

"Got you," he said quietly.

To Henry's surprise, within moments of moving alongside, the man was stroking the beast's underbelly and visibly the creature was calming down. Henry was impressed.

"Nay, I know this 'un," said the farmer. "It's one of Jessop's. Along at Fingland."

Fingland . . . Henry remembered it well.

"Help me get it into the paddock. I'll get me boots. We'd best get it back to 'em."

"Can I come, too? I mean, to Fingland?"

"Aye, you should be good at droving. But don't mucky yourself or the missis will play hell!"

Henry grinned. Ted Liddle was a good one to talk! The farmer had hurried out of the farmhouse still wearing his slippers. And Henry, not much better, was in long pants. Not new ones, but some cut-downs found by Mrs Liddle, a lot warmer than his old baggy shorts.

The farmer and Henry set off to walk to Fingland. The beast, calm again, moved placidly ahead.

Henry was intrigued. "How did you do that? I mean, rubbing it?"

"A gypsy taught me. Wisdom Joe they called him. From

Appleby. He could do owt with animals. I'll have to learn it you sometime."

They walked steadily until Henry with growing excitement began to recognise where they were. A familiar farm had appeared, one with blue gates and a lane at the side.

"I've been here before! When we were droving the geese."

"Was you now? Well this is Jessop's. Now turn the beast into the side or we'll find ourselves chasing it again."

Henry drove the bullock into the lane and shut the gates. The farmer knocked on the back door. He did not wait for an answer, calling as he stepped inside. Voices sounded and Henry, who recognised the pump where he got splashed, found himself meeting Mrs Jessop. It was the woman who had lost the baby.

"I knows you," she said. And then to Mr Liddle: "Kettle's on, Ted. You'll have a cup of tea?"

"Henry's just helped me catch your runaway. He's working for me missis and me."

"Well I'm grateful, I'm sure." Mrs Jessop gave Henry a smile.

But he was scarcely paying attention. He was looking at another figure that had come into the kitchen.

"Hello," said the girl.

They sat on the garden wall swinging their legs. She was in a blue check dress and had plaited her hair.

"You needn't have looked all *that* surprised," she told him.

"But you told me you didn't live here," said Henry.

"Well I do, for now anyway. I work for me aunt, helping with Uncle Tyson. He's got a bad back and can't move – and my name is Jenny."

"Mine's Henry," he told her.

She grinned, all freckles and tanned cheeks. "I know. I heard you. You yelled it loud enough! Anyway, why are you with the Liddles? They said you was going home or summat."

"I am. I mean, I don't know," he confessed. Then, rather like with the Liddles, he told her everything, even about their family photograph standing on the dresser.

He had finished and they fell silent. Somewhere nearby a hen was clucking softly.

"When did your dad die?" she asked eventually.

"Four years now . . . no, four years and two months."

He was shocked at how fast the time was going.

"My dad's a sailor. He's away a lot."

"It's step-fathers I don't like." said Henry.

"Then why doesn't your mum leave him? She could, easily. I know I would."

The thought shocked Henry. "She just wouldn't!"

"I shouldn't have said you smelt."

"Nay . . ." He grinned. "Happen I did."

"Will you come and see us again?"

"Aye, I might."

"Saturdays is best . . ." And then, more quickly: "You know, if it was *my* mum, I'd go and see her, even if he is nasty! Anyway, why don't she work somewhere else? She could work for my aunt. She could come here. I bet she could."

Henry walked back with Ted, his thoughts racing. The girl Jenny was all right, though she was wrong about his mother. His mother would never leave, not in a month of Sundays. As it was, he knew he ought to go and see her.

135

Within days there was the opportunity.

Ted Liddle sounded casual enough. "I'll be over at Silloth after some horse feed. Do you want a ride over?"

Henry, his arms full of hay, felt a moment of panic.

"You don't have to."

"Thanks, that is, I'm all right for now."

"Just thought you might fancy a trip. Anyway, don't fret on it, I isn't going till Tuesday."

Henry struggled with his thoughts. Why was everything so difficult? Should he go or not? The thought of Nathan always put him off.

Tuesday morning came and the farmer harnessed up the pony and got away soon after seven o'clock. Henry watched him go.

Nothing more happened at Ploughrigg for almost a month, not until the day Ted paid him four weeks' wages. It was an exciting moment.

As Ted explained: "Properly I'd not pay you till next hiring time, come Martinmas in November, but you and me's got a different arrangement, so you can have it monthly as we go. Happen you'll want to be letting your mother have some?"

Henry watched in awe as the farmer counted twenty shillings onto the kitchen table. A whole pound! Henry had never thought to possess so much. Only when the farmer had finished did the boy carefully slide two shillings back.

"For the goose," he explained.

Their eyes met in a smile.

25

Homeward Trek

He set off early in the morning and to his surprise at Fingland proper Jenny was in the front garden clipping a bush. It was hardly eight o'clock.

She saw his stick and the pack with its bread and cheese.

"So you are going home, then?"

"Yes. But I'll come back to the Liddles."

"I bet you don't! Where's your Moss?"

"They're looking after him, so I'll have to come back won't I? And there's me goose. Me goose is stopping too."

"Oh, I could go and see them for you. But what's made you change?"

Henry grinned. "Dunno, a proper wage I guess . . . I'm taking it to mum, so she can have . . . well, a holiday."

"A holiday?"

She was surprised.

"Well, sort of . . . yeah."

He knew it sounded wrong. Folk didn't have holidays. Not working folk. It was the first thing that had come into his head, but he wanted to do *something*. Perhaps his mother would just visit him at the Liddles. They had hinted she always could.

Jenny stood unsmiling, a girl in a long print dress, her hair down her back in a thick plait. But if she were unsmiling, her tone was enthusiastic "I'm glad, really glad . . . but wait, don't go. Not yet!"

She dropped the clippers into a basket and turned to the house. "I'll be back!" she called, hurrying to the door.

Henry waited wondering what she was up to and to his embarrassment when she returned her aunt was with her.

"He's just going," Jenny was explaining.

Mrs Jessop came out into the road. "Hello Henry, I hear you're walking home? It's a good long way."

"It'll happen be twelve miles, Mrs Jessop. I'll get there this afternoon."

"I'm sure you will. Those look good boots." She eyed them approvingly and he was glad he had cleaned them. "By the way, from what Jenny tells me would I be right in thinking your mother might think to move?"

"Nay . . ." The question took him by surprise. "Not as I know of. I mean I don't know."

Something had become more positive than he remembered saying.

Jenny stood alongside her aunt. "But she would, Aunt May. I bet she would if she got the chance!"

The woman looked at her, puzzled. "Nay lass, if she hasn't said so, I mean in so many words . . ."

Jenny stared desperately at Henry. She seemed to be willing him to say the right thing.

Mrs Jessop was aware of her concern.

"What does your mother do, Henry?"

The question always embarrassed him though he did not know why. Lots of people washed clothes to make a living.

"She washes things for folk, for some guesthouses, but mostly for folk."

Mrs Jessop looked interested. She knew the little town of Silloth well. "For guesthouses? And which ones might they be?"

But Henry couldn't remember all of them, except that at one there was Miss Partleton. He remembered her because she always gave him a thre'penny bit at Christmas.

The name seemed to register. "Doris Partleton? That'll be Robley's guesthouse. How tall is Miss Partleton?"

"She's only little," said Henry.

Mrs Jessop seemed satisfied. "She sounds the same. And Jenny tells me you are coming back to the Liddles."

"Aye. Me dog's stopping, and there's me goose."

Jenny was waving a newspaper.

"Show him your advert Aunt May."

Mrs Jessop smiled. "Lass, he won't want to be bothering with that just now."

But she took the paper and opened it up for him. It was a copy of *The East Cumberland News*.

"Page nine," said Jenny. She pointed to an advertisement.

Henry read it carefully.

Situations Vacant & Wanted
Wanted, a tidy, respectable housekeeper-companion
WOMAN
− Apply, Mrs Jessop, Blue Gates Farm, Fingland.

Henry caught a quick grin from Jenny, and half-glared half-smiled back at her. Flipping girls!

Hooking his bag onto the stick, he set it over his

shoulder. Time he was away.

His boots felt comfortable and solid. It was another sunny day and cool. It would be good to be out on the open road again

"Good luck!"

He did not answer. He kept moving. Strange, now that he thought about it he realised that all this time he hadn't really wanted to be going this way at all. Somehow things kept pushing him in the wrong direction. One thing he did know, though, his mother would never move from Silloth. *Silloth born and Silloth bred*, that meant a lot to Silloth folk.

26

Day Visitor

Henry stood nervously in Gregson's doorway. He was back in Silloth and he was soaked. It had been drizzling now for more than an hour. People came and went and then Lillian Sharples from the butcher's recognised him but she hurried past without speaking.

Across the road their house stood as if empty, though that did not mean anything. Nathan could be there unless he had gone to the pub. His mother would be in the kitchen and nothing would show out here at the front.

The door opened and a figure emerged. Henry shrank back. It was Nathan. Without glancing about him the man set off along the street. It was just what Henry had hoped but he waited until the man was out of sight before crossing over and letting himself in.

"Mum?"

There was a sound of something being put down in the kitchen. Elizabeth came hurrying out.

"Henry! Oh, thank the Lord! Where've you been? What's kept you away so long?"

She wept as they embraced. "I thought you were ill or something terrible had happened! And you – you are wet through!"

"Droving, mum. I've been droving. And I've got a job! Everything's all right. But what have you done to your arm?"

Her right arm was bandaged. She put a hand to it. "I fell . . . but you must get these wet things off. And you in long trousers! Ruben! Come down, it's Henry!"

Henry was surprised Ruben was not at school, but when he appeared Henry had a further surprise. An ugly bruise surrounded Ruben's left eye.

Elizabeth brushed aside Henry's question. "It was an accident. He'll go back tomorrow. Now get yourself changed or you'll catch your death of cold."

It was a joyful reunion. They sat by the fire, Henry drinking hot barley soup and telling how Torse had begged for food, and how a girl pumped water over him; and the fighting drovers, and Mr and Mrs Liddle and everything.

"I've even got me own goose. It's only got one eye, but it sees lots! And I've got a sheepdog! And he looks after geese just like that!"

They listened with scarcely an interruption and Elizabeth was conscious that Henry was growing up fast. There was a look of confidence that had not been there before; she could hear it in his voice. And here he was, almost fourteen, and in long pants!

"Mum . . ." said Henry at last.

And then he told her about Mrs Jessop. How she needed someone to live in, and what a good farm it was at Fingland.

"She's a lady, mum. Proper and kind." And then: "Mum, can't we leave here? Leave him?"

Ruben's face lit up. He looked more pinched than ever, but suddenly this sounded like a hope of escape. "Oh, mum, can we?" he pleaded. "Please. He'll hit me again, I know he will."

Henry stared. "Did he bash your eye?"

Ruben caught a look from their mother.

"Henry, I can't. You know I can't. There's clothes to wash, and there's Ruben's schooling. And the house. I can't just walk out . . . you know I can't."

Her face was wretched with anxiety.

"Did he?" Henry asked Ruben.

His brother nodded.

"And your arm mum?"

She tried not to, but she found herself weeping. Gently Henry held her to him.

"I can't just leave," she whispered. "When you weds it's for better or worse. It's what you promises."

Henry spoke softly: "But not if he hits you, mum. Or goes and bashes Ruben!"

"I just can't," she said. "We can't just give up here after all these years. Your father would never have wanted me to."

He knew she meant it. She had never let anyone down. She wouldn't.

Despite his mother's pleas, Henry decided to stay away this first night. He did not trust his feelings. He did not want to meet Nathan, not yet.

"I'll come tomorrow," he promised.

Elizabeth looked anxious. "But your bed's here. Where will you stop tonight?"

"Mum, I've got a pal. It's all right. I'll stop with him. Don't worry, I'll be back." He did not name the pal.

"Tomorrow," said Henry.

Ruben caught him at the door. "Your dog, it's not that same un is it? I mean, the one we found?"

Henry grinned. "Yes – Moss. He followed us, or really he followed me. And he's great with the geese!"

"Crikey!" Ruben's eyes shone.

"You'll see him! Now I gotta go."

He hurried away up the street.

At the pub Nathan had already heard. He heard from Lillian Sharples. "Are you sure?" he demanded.

"Yeah, it was him," said Lillian. "He were in Gregson's door spying. I didn't let on I'd seen him."

Lillian tucked her curls back under her hat.

"I'll go and find the little devil," said Nathan.

"I'll come with ya."

Nathan shook his head. "You get back to your job. Better she don't know about us."

"But it's half day. We're shut."

"I just told ya no, didn't I? Now shut up."

Henry would still be with her talking.

"I've summat to settle," he said.

But when he arrived at the house there was no sign of Henry. Ruben was upstairs and Elizabeth was busy ironing.

"I know he's been," glowered Nathan.

"Well he's not here now."

"Where's the brat got to? He's never paid up!"

"How do I know where he is? He didn't say! And don't call him a brat!"

She kept on with the ironing, avoiding trouble. Henry had told her about his job with the Liddles but had not mentioned his pay, nor did she expect anything for herself.

Nathan waited while Elizabeth was upstairs before he emptied the washing earnings out of the green teapot. He made sure the lid was back on before she came down.

"Six weeks away! He's not been with the geese all this time!"

Elizabeth sighed, tired of the endless bicker. "If you must know, he's got himself a proper job, on a farm."

"Oh, has he! Well he owes me money, woman!"

Elizabeth knew she had said too much.

"Don't you go bothering him. His wages is none of your business!"

We'll see about that, thought Nathan. He reached for his coat and scarf and slammed the door as he left.

27

Hunting Henry

He set off to search the dockyard. So Henry had been working had he! A whole month's pay likely.

The quay was empty. He barged open the door of the Doss. Empty again. A stink of heaped sacking and burned paraffin met his nostrils. Nothing moved. Nathan turned away and began walking the streets in hurried strides. He turned to the shore. An uneasy lash of the sea, but again no sign. Nothing by the Pierrots' stage. The brat was here somewhere. Nathan returned to the quay and paused. He'd beat him raw when he got him.

The day was going. In her kitchen Elizabeth fed Ruben and put Nathan's supper in the oven to keep warm. She was regretting she had mentioned Henry's job. Something bad would happen if he got to Henry first. She knew it, Nathan was getting worse.

Ruben saw her expression. "Henry will be all right, mum. Nathan won't find him."

Elizabeth sighed. "I want you upstairs."

"Mum!"

"Don't argue! Just go."

Better be sure that one of them was safe.

Ruben waited for thirty long minutes then crept down again and peered through a crack in the door. His mother was in the kitchen. He slipped out at the front and once in the street struggled into his jacket and hurried to the dock.

Outside the Doss he paused. No one in sight, just the harbour full of ships' spars.

"Henry?" He called softly, the door ajar.

There was little light. The hut looked empty.

"It's me."

He peered into the gloom.

"It's me, Ruben."

A heap of sacking stirred. Henry sat up. "Is he still there? He looked in."

"He's in town trying to find you. Mum says he's in a bad temper. He says you've got his money . . ."

Henry scrambled out. He was covered in grime.

"He's not getting any of it!" He sounded angry.

Ruben looked startled. "I didn't say he was."

"Sa'll right. I mean my wages is for you and mum. Now get back home."

"But aren't you coming?"

"Not till tomorrow. Like I said."

"Then I'll stop with ya."

"You won't! Mum's will find you've gone."

Ruben was dismayed.

"I'll come to the door with you," Henry offered, "but you've gotta stay at home tonight. She'll have the bobbies looking for you!"

They hurried along the dockside through the timber stacks, two half-seen figures. When they were least expecting it, they came up behind a man. They dropped to the ground.

"It's him!"

Nathan half-heard the scuffle and paused. Slowly he walked back, eying the heaps.

Henry gripped Ruben's arm and prepared to run for it but they were saved as something small and black ran out into the open. It was a cat. Something dangled from its mouth as it disappeared in among the stacks. Nathan grunted and turned away, sour faced. He'd find the boy later. The washing money jangled in his pocket and he retreated towards the warmth of a pub.

"Let's go," whispered Henry.

"The cat?"

"What?"

"It had summat."

"A rat. A dead un. It's allus catching 'em."

Ruben shivered.

The boys ran through chilly streets.

"It were a lucky rat for us," said Henry, "even if it was dead."

28

Nathan Strikes

Henry felt grubby and his clothes smelt. The Doss had been empty and stank of sweat and bacca smoke. Now he stood outside Robley's Guest House in the chill of a new morning. He needed an ally, a friend.

"Why, Henry," said Miss Partleton. "Goodness. Whatever is the matter?"

He had not meant to blurt it out, but he did. "It's Nathan," he told her miserably. "And me mum."

"Oh . . ." The little woman opened the door wider. "Come inside."

She led him into the kitchen.

"He's treating her badly isn't he?"

Henry looked wretched. "He's gone and hit her. And Ruben."

Miss Partleton showed no surprise. She waved him to a chair while she filled the kettle.

"She told me her arm was an accident."

"It wasn't. I want mum to get away, but she won't. I thought she would come and stop at my work spot or summat – there was a job in *The East Cumberland News* – but she just won't."

He knew he sounded desperate.

Miss Partleton shook her head. "She's tough is your mum. But we've got to do something. What the man needs is a warning."

Henry did not understand.

Miss Partleton drew in her breath. She took charge. "We'll have to face him with a few facts. You and me. And if he won't listen to us, then I'll go for Mr Parks."

Henry was surprised. "The policeman?"

"Certainly! Or he'll hit her again."

"Mum won't be wanting the police . . ."

"We'll see. First you must get cleaned up. No – I insist! You'll feel a lot better. I'll fetch you a jug of hot water."

When Henry emerged from the washroom Miss Partleton set down a plate of bacon and eggs. "Eat up, and then you need to sleep a bit."

"No, I can't stop . . ."

"Yes you can! You look exhausted."

She insisted. Yet she was gentle. She was only small but she had a way of getting things done her way.

"And you say you worked for May Jessop?"

"No – for the Liddles. But Mrs Jessop, I know her that's all. And the girl Jenny."

Miss Partleton nodded. "Now go and rest."

He slept heavily, until gone six o'clock, teatime. Only then did he prepare to go home.

Miss Partleton went to a basket and rummaged in some papers. "I'll have to come a bit later. We must decide what to do. And you can take this."

She gave him a copy of *The East Cumberland News*.

★★

150

The kitchen door crashed open. Nathan lurched in full of drink. His eyes fastened on Henry.

"So, the thief is back!"

He glared flush-faced across the racks of clothes that separated them.

"You owe me money, you brat!"

Henry was trembling but he stayed alongside the dresser. "I don't! The money's for mum!"

Elizabeth said: "Leave our Henry alone! His money is none of your business."

Nathan lurched again, seeking an easy way through. "So it's *our* Henry is it! Well I'll tan our Henry black and blue if he don't pay up!" He lunged, grabbing at Henry's hair.

"Got ya!"

But he was mistaken. Henry dropped to his knees and set off at a fast crawl through the clothes racks.

"Nathan, stop it!" screamed Elizabeth.

The man barged forward. "I'll kill him, I will!"

Everything tumbled in a tangle of clothes and wood.

"The fire! Mind the fire!" Elizabeth cried.

The man struggled through the mess. He got to Henry and knocked him flying against a wall.

"And what are these!" Nathan snarled. "Whose are the boots?"

"They're mine!" yelled Henry.

"Pinched 'em, have ya!"

Nathan grabbed Henry and wrenched them off him. "I'll teach you you little wretch!"

"Give 'em back! They're mine!"

"Get upstairs! And stop your damned lies!"

He thrust Henry out at the staircase door.

"Get to bed before I knock you there!"

Henry fled.

Nathan dragged aside a clothes rack.

Elizabeth stood aghast. "Nathan! Stop! What are you doing?"

"I'm teaching the brat a lesson."

He thrust the boots into the fire.

29

Escape

Henry lay awake in the dark nursing his bruised head. He was desperate to go down and rescue his boots.

Midnight was striking on a distant clock before steps sounded on the stairs and his mother came to bed. For some reason Nathan was still down in the kitchen. Why wasn't he coming up? Henry waited a while longer before he crept down and peered in.

His stepfather was slumped in the fireside chair snoring. Henry could smell beer and there was another fainter smell of scorching leather where Nathan's chair was close to the grate. Henry paused, afraid to wake him, then he got a better view of the hearth and stared in horror. Standing on the red hot coals in the middle of the fire was a glowing crimson pair of boots. They looked so perfect, almost as if they had been chiselled out of stone.

Anger welled within him. He must get them out! Before it was too late.

Risking waking Nathan he crept forward barefooted. The man's heavy breathing sounded in his ears as he crouched and reached for the hearth shovel. Trying not to tremble, he pushed it in under the boots and gently began to lift them.

It was a wasted attempt; the boots were a mere crimson image. They crumbled to pieces.

Somehow he got out of the room. Upstairs he wept bitterly into his pillow. He had never owned anything more precious than the boots, not even his little Union flag.

For a long time he stared at a patch of light on the bedroom wall then, exhausted, he fell asleep. Outside the great sky over the sea was clear and shone with a million stars. The night was quiet. Slowly the house began to fill with smoke.

A splintering crash of glass woke them.

Elizabeth found herself fighting for air. She realised instantly what was happening. Somehow she dragged the boys from their bed and got them onto the landing. "Downstairs!" she gasped. Thick smoke was everywhere. "Get downstairs!"

They were all coughing.

She propelled them before her and was shocked as they stumbled into the kitchen. A rack of washing was ablaze and the big window gaped open, shattered.

But the acrid smoke frightened her the most.

"For God's sake, *move!*" she gasped.

She paused long enough to grab a picture off the dresser, then gasping she dragged open the front door and they tumbled out in the open coughing until their eyes watered.

Behind them a dull red glow came from the passage. Without stopping to explain Henry broke away and ran off into the night.

"Mr Richardson, Mr Richardson!"

He banged on a door next to the fire shed.

"It's our house, Mr Richardson! Our house is on fire!"

Shouts and confusion! The street was waking. Soon grim-faced neighbours were racing up to form a bucket chain. If number 26 went, then 24 and 28 could easily be next. It had happened to others houses in the past. Everyone knew the danger.

The fire seemed to be mainly in the kitchen. As fast as buckets were filled, the water was pitched in through the back door into the blaze. It helped but everyone knew it was not enough.

Relief came. Shouts filled the front street. At the far end firemen came at a run, clutching a long pole towing the town's fire cart.

A muffled cheer sounded as the men arrived. Henry hardly dared to think they would put out the fire. But in minutes the hand pump was working and a fireman pushed in at the front door with a gushing hose.

"Here lads, wrap these round you!" Mrs Gregson was there and handed them thick blankets. "You can get yourselves inside our place and get warm."

But Henry stayed put. He wrapped the blanket round him and waited to see what happened.

An anxious time passed as the firemen pumped madly and slowly the fire did seem to be growing less fierce. For the first time the crowd in the street began to sense that the house might be saved.

And it was. A cheer sounded as firemen finally stopped pumping. Smoke and steam filled every room, but the fire was out.

It was now that they remembered Nathan.

Elizabeth's face was white. The last thing she wanted was another row.

"Where's he gone?"

They stared into the crowd looking for him.

"He was in front of us!"

"No he wasn't."

"Yes he was!"

But no one had seen him.

A terrifying thought struck her.

Henry watched in horror as the firemen pushed into the house and got to the kitchen. Nathan's body was found lying on the floor alongside the hearth. The smoke had killed him.

30

Time to Leave

Everyone was feeling cold. The shock of Nathan's death was etched in everyone's face.

A small figure came pushing through the crowd. "Oh, Miss Partleton," Henry cried. "It's Nathan."

"The poor man! I've just heard. But you can't stop out in the cold. You must come home with me."

Elizabeth was shivering. The fire and what it meant was only just striking her.

They stayed five nights at Miss Partleton's. Henry and his mother went to the funeral. Elizabeth wept. The man had not deserved to die.

And now, days later, Henry had a plan. He waited for the right moment before he told his mother.

For a while they put off visiting their old house, but now they did and Miss Partleton came with them.

Though everything was blackened the building was less damaged than they had expected. Firemen had boarded up the windows and Mr Gregson from opposite had a key for the padlocked door. But no one wanted to stay.

Henry got Ruben to one side and told him what to do.

Open mouthed, Ruben nodded and slipped away.

The moment had come.

"Mum, don't let's stop in Silloth!" Henry tugged at her sleeve. "Let's get away properly. Just the three of us – to Fingland, where I told you."

Elisabeth stared, startled. "Henry, we can't! You know we can't."

"Yes we can! Dad would have wanted it."

And now he was sure. All this time he had never really known what he wanted most. But now he did. "Fingland is really good," he told her warmly.

But she shook her head. "Henry, there's no way I am going to go and stay with strangers." She had never run away from anything and she would not start now.

Henry persisted. "We can stay with the Jessops, or with the Liddles where I work, I know we can! They are good folk. Fingland is *special,* I told you! And I've got my job. There's nowt here any more. How can you do folks' washing? Let's go while we've a chance."

"There's Ruben's schooling."

"Mum, there'll be a school."

"You do it, Mrs Gibbs." Miss Partleton pushed forward. "If that's May Jessop you are on about, she's a real bonny one! I knew her sister Joan. You'd be all right there!"

But Elizabeth did not change her mind. "I can't. There's all the burned washing to pay for. And, oh . . . some of it was yours!"

"Tush!" Miss Partleton waved a hand. "Nothing I can't stand. Get yourself away. Start again. I would!"

"Mum, we must!" Henry was excited. "We'll come back later and pay what we owe. And see, look at this advert. It's Mrs Jessop's."

He unwrapped a folded sheet of newspaper.

Elizabeth read it. And then she read it again.

Mrs Gregson came from across the road. "If you're going away I'll give Miss Partleton a hand. We'll be able to clear it a bit, till you can get back."

But Elizabeth knew she must stay. She did not know why exactly; it was something to do with not running away, with being responsible.

Despairing, Henry's hopes sank. He had seen his mother like this before. She could be stubborn at times. He had only one hope left but it was risky and it might not work. He began to button up his jacket.

"All right, then, mum." He spoke quietly, deliberately, matter of fact. This was his last chance. "If you don't want to come, I understand, but it means I'll have to go alone."

Elizabeth turned in alarm. "Go? Go where? What are you saying?"

"Back to Fingland, to my job." He smiled faintly. "At least I'll earn summat. The house here is no good anymore. Not now anyway."

She was shocked.

"You can't leave us! What about Ruben?"

Henry was blank faced and avoided her stare.

"I'll walk back there today. If Miss Partleton can see you are all right here . . . just for now."

Miss Partleton nodded at once, a knowing look in her face. "Yes, yes . . . of course I can."

"Then I'll go as soon as you are settled. Mum, we need the money."

Elizabeth's heart missed a beat. He was serious.

They embraced and for the first time she was filled with uncertainty.

A trundling noise sounded on the cobbles. Ruben arrived at a rush pulling Billy Dixon's handcart.

"He says we got to give it back or he'll kill us," panted Ruben excitedly, "but we can use it for now if we want. And we've to take care of the oil lamps and not break 'em."

It was the arrival of the cart that helped to change Elizabeth's mind. She looked at the boys' strained faces. Not a lot for them here, not in this blackened ruin, nor for her either.

"The cart?"

"He's only lent it," said Ruben to make sure she understood.

"But Finland . . . It's a long way."

"We'll have rests," insisted Henry. "Trust me mum. You've seen Mrs Jessop's advert. Finland is real good."

It was now that Elizabeth's final doubt went. All right, then. Yes! Why not? They were two good lads. Despite misgivings about leaving Silloth, for their sakes she would risk it.

"You're right! We'll do it!" she told them. And then, more certain: "I'll go!"

"It'll be all right," said Henry, his face bright and optimistic.

Elizabeth became practical. "Wait. Can't we see if there's anything worth saving?"

Henry and Ruben raced indoors. They avoided the kitchen hearth, climbing precariously up the staircase. They grabbed anything useful that was not badly burned, especially clothes.

They were surprised to find they had nearly filled the little cart. Mr Gregson padlocked the door of the house as they prepared to go. Several neighbours came across. "Good luck!

We'll miss you! Don't go and forget us will you?"

"I'll be back," Henry promised. "To help clear up." He was filled with a new confidence. He had become the young man of the family.

Elizabeth realised it too and was reassured. Just like his dad.

At Miss Partleton's insistence they called at her house where the little woman handed them a paper bag. "I thought you'd be wanting some food for the journey."

Elizabeth glanced at Henry. So Miss Partleton had known all along!

"It's just bread and cheese. And I've written this note to tell May Jessop I'll be across to see her myself one of these days. Perhaps you'd give it to her? We used to write one another long ago."

Shyly Henry held out his hand. "Miss P, thank you. For everything!"

The little woman winked the sliest of winks. "I knew something was going to happen!"

She was right, thought Henry.

They were off.

Miss Partleton helped with a starting push up to the end of the street.

"I know I'm not behaving sensibly," confessed Elizabeth. She had wrapped a shawl round her shoulders. They had a long walk ahead. She made sure she had wedged the silver frame under a blanket.

"You are, mum," said Henry, and she heard the confident ring in his voice. "You really are!"

"Yeah," said Rubin. For the first time in months he was feeling happy.

"Would you really have left me?"

Henry shook his head.

"Course not," he said.

But it had been a close thing.

Steadying the cart, they moved off.

Yes, Henry knew now what he wanted, and not just for himself, but for all of them. A fresh start. A new life. His hopes were pinned now on what happened at Fingland.

31

Ragged Caller

A knock sounded on Mrs Jessop's kitchen door. Henry set down his mug of tea and got up to answer it. His mother and Jenny were in the parlour with Mrs Jessop decorating. He had walked over from the Liddles soon after seven in the morning to repair a cupboard door. A whole year had passed since the blaze. It was as if he now had two homes, one at the Liddles, and the other here at Jessop's. He liked the thought.

"Hello . . ."

Tin in hand, waiting outside was a ragged man in an oversize coat.

The drover was as surprised as Henry. "Jaysus, boy! Is this you standing before me . . . the goose lad himself?"

Henry grinned in delight. "Torse! What are you doing here? Come inside!"

But the drover stared at the well-scrubbed kitchen floor and waved a blackened tin. "No, no, boy, I cannot be doing that."

"Come on in, it's all right," Henry reassured him. "We live here! Or my mum and Ruben do. Have done now for a year."

Still the drover shook his head.

"Thank you kindly, but I'll be glad of a drop of water, and if you have a small brew of tea you could be sparing for an old friend of the road . . . and bless us, here is your dog."

Moss was at his heels sniffing and wagging his tail.

"See, he remembers you," said Henry.

"So he does! And to think I never gave him a single biscuit in all the time we were on the road."

Henry filled up the tin with water and grabbed at the tea caddy as his mother came in.

"Henry?"

"Mum. It's my friend; it's Torse the Goose. Who looked after me, you know, all the way to Carlisle."

Elizabeth took in the ragged figure and her face lit up. "Why bless us, Mr Torse. Won't you come in? Henry has told me all about you."

The warmth of her welcome touched the drover. Overcoming reluctance, he tugged off his muddy boots and stepped inside. And in a moment they encouraged him to take a seat, and he was perched on a chair gratefully supping a mug of sweet tea when Mrs Jessop came through to hear his adventures.

They filled his mug with more tea and he was very polite, saying how he would never have managed the geese half so well had Henry not been with him, and now another year had gone. He had walked a fresh lot of birds to Carlisle, quite alone this time, with only the two hundred to manage, because the market was not so good this year. And *how* Henry had grown! And what a pleasure it was to meet the boy's own sweet mother, and how it was he missed Henry on the road, the Irish Road, always so helpful and . . .

When the drover left, the two of them walked up to the

164

little gate together.

"That man, your step-da," said Torse. "Is he not here?"

Henry gave him a bleak look. "He died . . ."

"Oh. Did he now?"

"He'd sort of had a lot to drink."

He said nothing more. The memory though it still hurt was slowly fading.

They passed a fat goose.

"That one's mine," said Henry proudly. "You know, the one you gave me."

Torse stopped to stare. His eyebrows rose in surprise. "No! Is that so! The very same?"

"Only one eye," said Henry.

"So it has! And you never put the bird in the oven!"

"No. But I sold it, at first, and then . . . well, I bought it back. Anyway, guess what! It helped me find a job, *and* a proper place here for mum and Ruben."

"Why, boy, that is good, that is!"

The drover stared at the goose again as if to make sure it really was there. "And you've kept it all this time and not put it in the oven!"

Torse's face broke into a rare look of delight and momentarily his air of loneliness seemed to fall away. He peered at Henry with his wild eyes.

"Now boy, did not Torse tell you how walking the geese would be the making of you?" He smiled, slightly toothless, pleased at how right he had been. "I told you, now, didn't I!"

"You did," acknowledged Henry.

"And you never did believe me, did you!"

"I always wanted to," Henry told him sincerely. "More than anything I always wanted to. And now I do."

They smiled at one another.

The drover patted him on the shoulder, firmly, and this time it seemed the right thing to do.

"I'm going to miss you, boy. Torse is going to miss you, he is."